The Story of Maryhill Youth Club

D1150958

Motto

*"Service is the rent we
pay for our room on Earth"*

by
Jay Muirhead

MARYHILL YOUTH CLUB
Incorporating
WOODSIDE LADS CLUB
And
MARYHILL CLUB
1933 - 1965

ISBN: 978-1-905787-70-8

PRINTED AND PUBLISHED BY
For The Right Reasons
60 Grant Street
Inverness
IV3 8BN
fortherightreasons@rocketmail.com or 01463 718844

In loving memory of my grandparents
James and Helen Muirhead.

Who devoted all of their adult lives to
helping young people.
Who inspired so much in others.

And to my dad, Robert (Bobby)
Muirhead,
who still devotes his life to helping others.

With Love

Jay x

All proceeds of this book are donated to For The Right Reasons charity to help support their youth programme and the continued development of their youth work.

ACKNOWLEDGEMENTS

The research for this book was taken from local news and national newspaper archives, web pages, documentation, letters and cuttings of articles collected from 1932-1992.

Evening News	Glasgow Evening Times	The Bulletin
Glasgow Herald	The Evening Citizen	The Citizen
The Glasgow Times	The Daily Record	The Daily Mail
The Daily Express	The County Reporter	The Sunday Mail
The Sunday Post	Scottish Sunday Express	The Gazette
The Lanarkshire Gazette	The Peoples Journal	The Times
Daily Mirror	The Weekly News	Sporting Record
The Lennox Herald	The Pathfinder Magazine	

CONTENTS

CHAPTERS   PAGE

1992   The end and the beginning   7
1907   The beginning   9
1933   The Woodside Lads Club   15
1934   The Sunbeams   17
1937   The church closes its doors.   23
1938   Maryhill Youth Club   29
1939   The War   34
1940 - 41 The war work begins   38
1942   The work continues   45
1943   The Valley Gang   49
1943   Letters in the post   55
1944   Pioneering in progress   59
1945   The war ends and the club continues to   65
           advance.
1946   Something old, something new   73
1947   A little rest   81
1948   Basketball, the sport and the Maryhill Club   87
1949   Maryhill Club invades Europe   94
1950   Larger than Life   103
1951 -53   A quiet time   114
1954   Out with the old, in with the new   121
1955   The birth of the teenager   128
1956   By popular demand   135
1957   Alone we stand   143
1958 -59   National heights   147
1960- 65   The demise of the Maryhill   155
1950- 65   Our Club Members   167
1967 -70   Sounds familiar   181
1971 -80   The Servades are born   188
1981- 89   The decline of an era   196
The ending   204

1992
THE END OF THE BEGINNING

June 19th 1992 and everyone was gathering at 40/2 Cook Road, Haldane, Balloch. Helen Muirhead sat quietly in her arm chair. Her image was one of perfection, at only 5 feet in height, with a petite figure and her short grey hair immaculately curled under her black hat. She was a picture of elegance and grace in her black coat. Her gloved hands clasped her bag which was poised correctly on her lap. Sitting perfectly straight with her legs tucked to the side of the chair, the flawless poise for a lady. Surrounded now by her family, the silence echoed loudly around the small living room. This would be a day that would be fixed firmly in everyone's heart.

Robert Muirhead stood at the fireplace with his arms crossed. He was average height for a man, but at 52 years he had the physique of an athletic man. Looking over at Helen, her unmoving grace disturbed him. Placing his hands in his pocket, he walked across the room and glanced out of the window, his thoughts lost for a few moments in the buzz of the traffic. He gave a small wave of recognition to someone outside before turning towards Helen. He spoke softly, "The car is here, mum."

Helen rose from her chair and nodded. "It's time," she said and slowly made her way out of the house followed by her son Robert and his wife, her two grandchildren and their partners. Helen's heart was breaking; they had been together so long, done so much and now it had ended.

Helen walked towards the black Daimler her head held high. There was something Victorian in her manner, the saying 'a stiff upper lip' comes to mind, we knew her so well.

The Muirhead family, to anyone watching, must have seemed devoid of emotion, but in reality each one of them hurt deeply. Helen and her husband had always been private people and believed strongly that emotional and physical demonstration were not for public display, and their influence and views were reflected within their family unit, even down to the grand children. The pain and loss of her husband was personal and she would mourn alone, behind closed doors. The family entered Cardross crematorium and were greeted by a young man who escorted them to their seats. The walk down the chapel aisle seemed exceptionally long but they took comfort from the familiar faces of friends and loved ones who had come to mourn.

Iain Miller, the family minister, had become a good friend with the Muirheads. Over the years they had often helped him with raising money for his church, and now it was his turn to give his service. He began to speak, "We are gathered here today, to pay tribute to Jimmy Muirhead, to rejoice in his life." The words 'rejoice in his life' whirled around my head. Watching the coffin as it disappeared behind the curtain, I realized that it was maybe the final curtain on his physical body but not to his memory.

James had, since the very beginning, collected letters and newspaper clippings which were arranged into two large volumes. This is his story, his love of Maryhill, its people, his work, his passion.

James had a vision. He wanted to give the youths of Maryhill an inspiration for life, keep them off the streets and keep them out of the local gangs. He wanted to give them hope for a better future. He wanted to spread that hope and future everywhere and he came so close. It all began in 1907.

Maryhill

1907
THE BEGINNING

It was the eleventh of November 1907 to be exact and today had been just like any other day in the streets of Maryhill. People were going to and from their work and the wains were playing on the street. The clouds in the sky were grey and heavy with rain which made the tenements of Maryhill more dark and intimidating than normal.

There was one family who lived in 4, Garrioch Drive, Maryhill, Glasgow. Robert Muirhead was an ordinary working class man. The last twenty four hours had been quite stressful. As he sat down in his arm chair still dressed in his work trousers, braces over his tattered, varnish stained shirt, he hadn't even removed his flat cap, but he had managed to pour himself a small glass of whisky. He wasn't a drinker but today was special after all. Robert had met his wife, Jane Sinclair, eighteen months ago, when he had been working with his father up at the big house owned by the Sinclair Family. Mr Sinclair was to Robert a typical rich upper class snob, who never spoke to the hired hands. However his daughter, Jane, had stopped briefly to talk to him, much to her father's distaste and anger which he had conveyed rather nastily.

Robert spent the next few weeks at the big house, and over that period he had spent time with Jane and very soon they were in love. Jane's parents tried to keep them apart, but they took every opportunity they could to meet. Mr Sinclair found himself confronted with the prospect that his daughter wanted to marry this man. Horrified that his daughter could consider such a union to a man well beneath their status, a common carpenter, her father begged her to reconsider. When he realised that his daughter was actually going to marry this man, he severed all ties with her, emotionally and financially.

The couple married quietly. In those times it was expected that women married young and families were started immediately. Jane had fallen pregnant three months into the marriage. Robert was a skilled joiner and boat builder, working in the family business. During the night Jane had gone into labour. Husbands weren't allowed to be present at the birth so Robert was sent to work. After what seemed like days of labour to Robert, his wife had given birth to a son, James Muirhead.

Robert and Jane had no idea that their son was going to grow into a wonderful man whose love and determination would influence the lives of hundreds of people and their futures. Walking through the streets of Maryhill in 1907 and for some years to come, it was common to see kids in the streets with their grubby smiling faces. There were no play stations or DVDs like we have now. These kids had imaginations and inventive minds and they seemed quite happy. Many adults who grew up playing in the streets and the back courts of Maryhill described their life as hard and money was short.

George Macmillan grew up in Maryhill. This now elderly man, was sitting on his chair with a smile, chuckled his way through his childhood stories. "We'd aw played the gether," he said with a big cheesy grin. "I have fond memories o' Maryhill as a wain." As he spoke he gently rested his head against the back of his chair, a warm smile on his face as he drifted into his memories. He was caught in his own childhood. There was an expression of contentment which spread over his face, and the recollections of his childhood certainly weren't all bad. Just listening to his stories, the freedom of playing in the street, how he and his friends jumped over the walls of the back courts even though it could be quite a drop on the other side, but there was something more about this man's childhood. The more he spoke, twinges of envy were growing. Never would we know the days of the trams, the concert parties or the dance bands. Our children would never experience the hours of playing safely in the street in the way our parents did, nor would they ever experience games such as beaver, kick the can or peerie.

Caroline Haldane grew up in Maryhill. "We always played on the street, there was nowhere else to go, and my mother wouldn't let me stay in unless I was ill," she said and shook her head before continuing. "There wasn't much to do inside anyway," she smiled.

"Were your parents very poor?" was the question asked. The look on her face said it all. She replied rather indignantly, "Poor folk were other people, I didn't think I was poor. I didn't know what toilet rolls were or what a table cloth was or what it was to live in a house with carpets. God, we didn't get a T.V. until 1959, but I was happy." She paused for a moment as if in thought before she continued, "It was hard to miss what you didn't have." There was truth in these words. Often as a parent the more you give your children the more they expect. These people had fond memories, but the reality was there was nowhere for the children to play other than the street or the closes and someone would always be complaining about the noise. James Muirhead led a relatively normal childhood and was educated at Hillhead High School. He was very keen on sports and Highland dancing for which he won many medals, and in particular for sword dancing. He had a passion for dance, music and for writing, and a love of the arts. His father often remarked that his mother too had passion for such nonsense.

Kilted young James

11

His father didn't approve of such things, and certainly was not going to encourage his son to pursue such upper class activities. It was to be a good proper job for James, none of these high falutin ideas above his station. When he was just fourteen years old life dealt him a hefty blow. His mother died.

Robert loved his wife, and at times he wished he could afford the finer things in life for her, or someone to help keep house. Jane was always a lady. She never complained and took on her household tasks without a grumble. Housework in those days was physically hard work, floors would be scrubbed by hand, rugs had to be beaten, clothes were hand washed, and then it would be time to prepare the evening meal.

Jane had gone into the kitchen to start the cooking. Working away she knocked over one of the heavy pans which came crashing down on her foot. Later that evening, looking at her bruised foot with its deep cut, she shook her head at her own stupidity. But there was no reason to go to the doctor. You had to pay for the doctor and after all it was only a bruised foot, but that wasn't to be the case. The foot festered and the infection spread rapidly and death followed shortly after. The cause was septicaemia which unfortunately was a common cause of death in those times.

Robert worked hard to provide a home for James, and kept him at school as long as he could. James did well and studied hard, but he didn't want to join the family business. Instead he wished to become a quantity surveyor. His father insisted he joined the family business so James secretly wrote this letter to a local firm:

Robert Muirhead

12

'John Alexander Wilkie,
Surveyors and Valuer
J.A.Wilkie Esqr

Dear Sir,

I hereby make application for a position in your
office, to serve my time at the measuring. I am 15 years of
age, and I was educated at Hillhead High School.
I can assure you I will do the best I can to learn the
measuring, and be of what service I can while in your
employment.

Yours respectfully,
James Muirhead'

James commenced his apprenticeship on the 15th January 1923, much to Robert's sadness. The apprenticeship lasted until 1928 and he continued to work for three more years with the firm before leaving for a more commercial appointment.

James had a sharp mind and a thirst for knowledge, which he pursued with much passion. He was soon attending evening classes at the School of Social Studies at Glasgow University, whilst also working with a charity in a voluntary capacity at the City of Glasgow Society Of Social Service. There were several of these society offices within the Glasgow area. This organisation sought funding on a private level as there were no government or council grants, nor was there a welfare state. Social work hadn't even been created as we know it now. This charity, like many of its kind, provided clothes and sometimes financial support to those who weren't working, and possibly to help support those who were too old to work or were on a very low income with tiny mouths to feed. The City Of Glasgow Society Of Social Service still exists today. It is still privately funded and is still supporting those who need its services.

Every Sunday, as a child, James attended church and continued to attend well into his adult life. Churches in these times also provided help within their communities, with clothing, food and much more. Eastpark Church of Scotland was James' church where he became their Sunday school teacher. By 1934 he was their Sunday school superintendent and also clerk to the deacon's court of Eastpark church.

His association with the charity and the church served to heighten his awareness of the situation around him; groups of youths on the street with no money and nowhere to go. Time after time he heard stories about youths on the street developing talents that led them to gang activities of crime leading to imprisonment. James was sure if he could provide a venue for them and interact with these youths he could make a difference. So with little money and a big heart he rented an old shop in Garscube Road for £7 10/- (£7.50) a year.

1933
THE WOODSIDE LADS CLUB

The shop had been closed for a long time, and as James gazed at his surroundings he shuddered at the grim grey tenements of Maryhill that looked so very hostile as they loomed above. It was a depressing backcloth for his visions and his plans for this little corner shop, but then again where else would Jimmy start? After all this was the very place that the children he wanted to help lived. He was on their home turf now and James was here to stay.

For a long time he had been concerned about the lack of positive attention that was being given to the young people in Maryhill, and now he was taking his first steps to change things.

The little shop was daunting on the outside, but inside it had hope and promise. His vision saw past the paint peeling from the doors and the wall paper that was falling from the cracked and tired walls. Even the puddle of rain water on the floor didn't dampen his hopes. James set to work, calling upon his father's skills, and soon the interior of the building was given a new lease of life. He managed to get an old punch bag and some skipping ropes. Physical exercise was to be the basis of his work. First he would teach them to expel their anger and frustration and then, channelling this anger, he would instil a positive discipline and structure through sports such as wrestling, boxing and football.

James was aged just 27 years old and unsure of what to expect. He eagerly awaited his opening night. Walking into Garscube Road that first night, he was nervous and excited. He had already affiliated his club to the Glasgow Union of Boys Clubs. With all his heart he felt that, even if only one boy turned up, then his efforts would not have been in vain. To his delight eighteen young boys arrived. Over the next four years the club grew in numbers until there were nearly fifty members. He begged people for equipment for the club and persuaded the army to help out with P.T instructors. He even managed to persuade others who were experienced in boxing and wrestling to give their knowledge and skills as well as their time, free to the boys' club.

James himself taught Highland dancing and sword dancing. All too soon the lads' club activities began to grow.

Newspaper sketch of James

1934-1937
THE SUNBEAMS

James was delighted with the progress of the Woodside Lads' Club. It had been a good positive start, but what of the other younger children who were just as susceptible to a future of gang life and crime? His answer was intervention at an earlier age and that would be a more positive approach to the current situation.

Approaching the church committee, he suggested the idea of an open doors policy. He wanted to open the church doors to all the younger children, not just for the children whose families were church members. The committee decided that, as an experimental venture, he could use the church hall once a week, but not Sunday.

James set to work. Happy Hour was what he called the Monday night meetings. Sessions would begin and end in prayer, and he would include interesting talks, discussions and singing. It was from this activity that he built the foundations and developed his concert party.

During the first month it was obvious that the children were curious. They came in large numbers. However, several months down the line, James found that there were so many children coming he was having to close the doors half an hour before the club started.

In October 1934, the minister of the church had been at a wedding. Passing the church hall he was delighted to see so many children outside the building waiting for Happy Hour to begin. The minister wrote James a letter. He was pleased with James' work. Since Happy Hour had begun the Sunday school numbers had risen to over thirty.

'My dear James,

I was at a wedding in the vicinity at 7pm last night and was delighted to see hundreds of children waiting to get into your 'happy hour'. You have splendid organisational abilities. I will do all I can to help you and get help for you.

Please let me know any or all the schemes you have in mind. This is good work.

Yours sincerely,
George Macarthur'

Original poster

Helen Waddell was asked to assist with Happy Hour. Like James, she was a Sunday school teacher in the same church and she wanted to help. Like many others in the church she had heard of James' work and thought it was wonderful. From the first night they worked together, it was the perfect partnership.

The concert party was doing well and in 1936 they were ready for their first charity concert. James placed this notice in the local shop window.

A
GRAND
ENTERTAINMENT
(In aid of the Necessitous Children's Holiday Camp Fund)
By the
Eastpark Sunday School Sunbeams
In the
MARYHILL BURGH HALL
On
FRIDAY, 20th MARCH, 1936 at 7.30pm

The concert programme consisted of six songs performed by the entire company, with fifteen acts and sketches by small groups or individuals of the concert party. From that moment, their presence was requested to sing on various occasions in church and their performances were outstanding.

That same year, James entered his Sunbeams into the Glasgow District Music Festival. They were the only junior entrants to the contest. The music committee considered the Sunbeams to be too young to perform. They had performed at several charity events, and were loved by the people who had seen them. The Sunbeams were finally permitted to perform their act, 'Six who pass while the lentils boil.'

James had also started a Sunday school choir which he incorporated the Sunbeams into. In 1937 James put on an operetta with his choir. The picture in a local paper held the title **'Sweet little Maryhill singers in pretty operetta.'** The reporter wrote: - *'The Sullivan operetta 'Sisters Three' was performed with much success by the sweet voiced members of a Maryhill parish church junior choir. Britannia was impressive and the boys and girls who filled the Scottish roles showed creditable knowledge of Scottish mannerism.'*

Junior choir and Sunbeams

Over the next year the Sunbeams grew in number. Helen had proved to be a valuable asset to the Monday night group and James asked her to help out with the boys' club. The pair worked between the Happy Hour and the Woodside Lads Club.

There was unease growing within the church community and soon it was brought to James' attention that there was an increasing concern surrounding these children. But he didn't falter and continued with his work. Helen was behind James a hundred percent. She shared his compassion for the children, and believed in his visions, so it was no surprise to those who knew them, when on the 23rd of July 1937 James and Helen were married in a small intimate service.

Happy couple

Before they were married, the young couple looked around for somewhere to live. James had lived all his days in Maryhill and this is where he wanted to stay. Unfortunately there was a lack of property that they could afford in Maryhill. They managed however to purchase a house in a new development at 1, Hillside Avenue, Bearsden.

When the young couple returned from their brief honeymoon, they discovered James' father, Robert, waiting for them. He assumed that he would be living with his son and his new bride. The young couple felt that they could do nothing more but allow him to stay.

Wedding party

1937-1938
THE CHURCH CLOSES ITS DOOR

September 1937. James was preparing the speech he was to deliver at that evening's church A.G.M. He had been very pleased that some of the children from his Monday night group were becoming regulars in the Sunday school. At first the response was good but now these children were unhappy and were slowly removing themselves from the church. When James asked what the problem was, every one of them complained that the other Sunday school teachers had put them out of the play hour which was run for Sunday school children. James was horrified and approached one of the Sunday school teachers asking if it was true. The reply was, "Do you think we are going to play with your dirty little hooligans." Tonight at the meeting, he was going to remind them that they could not be selective in whom they preached God's word to, or who they should help. This was his original speech.

'Being merely a layman and not a member of the honourable profession of which a number sit before me, and to whom notes are unnecessary, I shall use mine, for without notes and in dealing with such a subject I might wander, and tend to create what one might call a chaotic atmosphere. And as this talk is unorthodox, I will treat my subject in the time-honoured orthodox manner and in the ministerial method of firstly, secondly and last, brethren, and I promise not to make lastly as long as the rest of my talk.

Well, to get on with the subject, my first question to you, are the Sunday schools of today cutting any ice? Have we idly wandered into a cul-de-sac, by being content with the knowledge we have a Sunday school, and that our reverend figureheads are able to assure the presbytery year after year that they have so many scholars on their rolls. Yes friends we have found it easier to do that, to get along any way rather than face some good hard work.

Are we carrying out the true and best traditions of our Sunday school by forgetting about the boy and the girl outside our school? "Yes," I hear that cry of indignation from my audience "we have tried to recruit our schools." Perhaps you have friends, and yet, how can you answer the question that there are hundreds of boys and girls around every school in the north west union, literally untouched by any church organisation, and my contention tonight is that if it is anyone's job to remedy this it is surely the Sunday school's. But perhaps I have made a mistake in saying so; it may be that the Sunday school teacher of 1937 is too respectable to go 'slumming'.

One Sunday school tried this with success, until one day a few of the children approached the superintendent complaining that they had been put out of the primary play-hour, and on the primary leader being asked about this, her reply was "do you think we are going to play with your dirty little hooligans?" If that is the outlook of the genuine Sunday school teacher of today, then I may as well stop now before you decide that I've got bats in the belfry. But I don't believe that the real Sunday school teacher will have nothing to do with the so called little hooligans. We have a God-given privilege to teach the children the love of God, and we were never meant to stop because the children were dirty. Use your influence and very soon the dirty child will be one of the cleanest in the school. God doesn't confine himself to one congregation or one parish; why should we, who are trying to help in his work?

I can imagine someone ready with the question, the old excuse, "we have no time to do any more." I think if we enthuse in the proper spirit, and see something worthwhile doing, we will find that extra time, as S.S.T. we have to rise to the heights of our calling so that we may pass on the religion of our fathers to the men and women of tomorrow. And the question I hear next amongst my audience "how are you going to get the children to school." By the usual method of canvassing and that has already failed. Well here's where my unorthodoxy comes in. I don't believe in canvassing. I have tried it in two districts in the North West with different organisations and it failed miserably.

There is only one way and that is contact. I have tried out a scheme for two years now and it has been a hard fight. I have named it 'Happy Hour' but many people prefer to call it the rabble. We meet in the hall every Monday evening where we have a prayer, a hymn, thereafter a lantern lecture, a concert party or interesting talk. I have never canvassed, the meeting is open to all boys and girls and many evenings we have closed the door half an hour before starting time, with 400 children in the hall and 200 outside clamouring to get in, and over 50% of these children have no church connection whatsoever. The scheme is by no way perfect, but I have succeeded each year in drawing at least 30 boys and girls into the Sunday school without compulsion.

If every school in the North West could only get 20 or 30 children per year then our worthy secretary would not have to complain at the A.G.M. of the dropping numbers.

Now I know I have got myself into bother. Some friends are ready to jump to their feet with the old argument "you are getting those children by bribery and corruption." Yes they are coming originally out of sheer curiosity I admit, but I defy anyone to criticise a method that draws the children within the atmosphere of the church by curiosity. So were they who followed Christ in the streets of Jerusalem and into the wilderness, but with what results?

My second point is very essential. It is staff. Remember I am not dealing with classes on a Sunday, but simply with the problem of reaching out for those children outside the fold. I have only a dozen I can depend on in this venture, but I find it quite sufficient. While I'm at one with the modern Sunday school I sometimes think that too much is given to technique, discussion, training classes etc.

One certainly must be sufficiently trained, but if it is not the proper person who is trained, then it is simply a waste of time. In other words, what I mean is, training classes, conferences etc. are all pure substitutes for consecrated personality. To carry out this big venture we have to revert to faith. We Sunday school teachers have that. Some people think faith is believing about Christ, or swallowing something that has no meaning for them, and by doing so receive a nice brown paper parcel with salvation written on it. But faith is not staking your whole life in doing some job, going all out and daring everything for the advancement of Christ's kingdom. Jesus was a pioneer. He expects his followers to be pioneers. You have the chance to be pioneers right now in this challenge I am throwing out to you tonight. Remember this one point: you can't be a Christian in a sentry box.

Yet we find Christian workers excusing themselves from being pioneers simply because they are bound up in systems, codes and customs. It all depends on how much you're willing to pay and/or be laughed at. Christ does not lay down the law. He is not the task master, but he tries to make us so sure of God that we will have the faith to go forward gladly and do that little extra for him. If we Sunday school teachers can make that little extra effort this session, no matter how small our staff may be, if we bind ourselves in the greatest tie of this fellowship, the gift of prayer. If we bring God to the field of our consciousness, then the atmosphere we bring to our work will bring those who are standing looking-on into the fight with us and make us achieve that which at the present we think impossible.

And lastly friends I will be short as I promised. We all recognise that there is a desperate need and an unparalleled opportunity today for new effort to sweep through our schools. Our numbers are going down year by year. We are failing to overtake the mission work which we should be doing, but as I said before, Christ tries to make us so sure of God, that in everything we are willing to put our hands to for him he will give us the faith to go forward without a tremor.

The spirit has risen
From the narrow letter which kept
Men's thoughts in a prison
Where they struggled and languished or
slept
And now we can soar high above
All the creeds
But the credo of love.'

This powerful speech was to make no difference to the church committee; they would not see his passion or his vision, their eyes and hearts were closed.

A week had passed since the church meeting. As James was getting ready to leave the house for work, lying on the hall table was the post. One letter in particular caught his eye. Opening the letter he surveyed its contents with great disapproval and anger. "How dare they?" he thought, throwing the letter down in disgust.

The church committee had decided that they no longer felt that Happy Hour was the way forward. They had to think of their members, who considered these children as repulsive, and no longer wanted to be associated with these dirty little creatures with their torn clothes, especially in their own church premises. Happy Hour would cease immediately and James was to remove these children from the church premises at once. James felt his stomach lurch. He was not a man who easily rose to anger, but at this moment he was so angry and horrified at the church's reaction towards these children who had worked so hard. In the beginning most of them had never seen a musical instrument let alone play one and now they were a concert party. If only the church members would come to Happy Hour and see these children dance and sing and listen to them belt out their tunes, surely the church would be moved by the enthusiasm and the energy of these young children. For weeks he fought for the Sunbeams, pleading with the church but to no avail, and James was left with only one option, he could do nothing else but to adhere to the church's wishes.

Saddened by the rejection from the church, the church he had always attended and of which he was their superintendent. This was against everything he had been taught and he had no idea what was he going to tell the children, feeling that the church had gone against their teachings. James remembered these words that Jesus had said, "Bring the little children unto me." With these words in his thoughts he resigned from the church in January 1938.

That month the church published their Eastpark Church Life and Work supplement magazine. This was a regular publication to inform members of meetings and events. So it seemed only natural to write regarding James' resignation, his years of service to the church and all of his good work. This is the content of the article.

> *'Within recent days changes have taken place in the administration of the Sunday school. Mr James Muirhead, whose name is synonymous with Sunday school work, has found it necessary to terminate his activities in Eastpark church.'*

James pleaded with the church to allow him permission to keep using the hall for the children. He offered to rename the club and inform the parents that the club would no longer be affiliated in any shape or form to the church. He was refused; the church had closed its doors.

The hardest thing was watching the children's faces as he told them that there was to be no more Happy Hour, or performances from the Sunbeams.

1938
MARYHILL YOUTH CLUB

James was not to be discouraged. There was still the Lads Club and there were nearly fifty members who depended on him. Making his way that night along the dark streets into Garscube Road there was heaviness in his heart. He was in conflict with himself. He had given these children a purpose and hope, and in an instant he had taken it away from them. He would not make that mistake again.

Arriving that night at the Woodside Lads Club was to change his life and his club forever. To his surprise there were his Sunbeams waiting at the door. These children were not going to be told that they could not perform anymore. With a smile James opened the doors to his club with great delight as he accommodated them all in his little shop. It wasn't ideal. That first night was extremely cramped but he had a resolve; they would just open more nights a week, providing more space and the possibilities of more activities. After a few weeks of consultation with Helen, they developed their plan. Within a few weeks it was opening six nights a week and the club was generating more interest. Helen was now running the girls' section of the club under James' supervision, with keep fit, first aid training and nursing of the sick.

It was quite common to see little faces peering through the windows of the club as they watched James and Helen put the others through their activities. Very soon these little faces were finding their way through the door to join the club. Eventually there were just as many girls as boys so James renamed it the Maryhill Youth Club.

From the word go the motto of the club was, 'To serve others.' James believed that, 'Service is the rent we pay for our room on earth.' James had the Sunbeams touring Glasgow raising money for charities and churches. Since that first night they arrived at his little shop, James had been offering the services of these performers. He never once charged a fee for these performances, and only occasionally did the club receive a donation or monies to help with travelling.

P.T. Team

The only way clubs and groups could survive was through donations from the public or generous business men. James established quickly a concert for club funds and from that moment onwards the Maryhill Youth Club hosted an annual display of all their activities including entertainment from the

Sunbeams. At these times he would be hopeful of donations. Every penny was gratefully received but they didn't go far.

James wasn't going to let these children down again, so he just worked harder as a quantity surveyor to help meet the extra funds that the Maryhill Youth Club needed to survive.

He believed whole-heartedly that any organization or club that helps people to develop, should avoid catering for their entertainment or amusement. Usefulness is an essential item, doing things both to help yourself and others is an important factor.

James had ability, he worked well with children. He was gaining more experience by the second but he still had teething problems to overcome. He found that some of the youths just wanted to be in the concert party, so he decided that all club members had to take part in at least one activity to be considered for the Sunbeams, and that included the original members of the concert party.

This did not go down well with some of the youths, they grumbled and groaned, but James stayed firm in his decision. If you wanted to stay in the club you had to abide by the rules. One chap in particular was unhappy about the whole situation. That was Eddie. He was about fifteen and did not like being told what he could and could not do and he voiced his opinion. "Mr Muirheid, that's no fair, I kin play the mouthy but I canny dae a burlywulk." The reply was more of what later became the philosophy in their club work; it wasn't about how good you were, if you couldn't do a forward roll it wasn't important, but to work as part of a team, be committed to what you did, give it all you had with a smile on your face, then you had earned the right to be in the team.

The Muirheads taught self worth and confidence; not only did you respect your elders but you respected yourself and the person beside you.

It was late October and Helen wasn't feeling quite herself. It was the terrible tiredness that was making life difficult. At first she had considered the possibility that with the rapid growth of the club, every day was full steam ahead, six days a week. She was certainly overstretching herself, especially now that they were transporting children all over the place. There were competitions for the boxing and wrestling teams not to mention the new cycling section, the Maryhill Wheelers, who were competing in cross country cycling events, as well as the Sunbeams who were increasingly more in demand, touring Glasgow raising money for different organisations. Then there was still the everyday running of the club, paper work, costumes to make and, of course, routines to put together as well as running a home and looking after her husband and father-in-law.

But the honest truth was she was beginning to feel quite ill and was losing weight. One night James returned home early from work to find Helen lying on the kitchen floor. She tried to reassure James that she had just fainted but he was having none of it, especially after what had happened to his mother and at once sent for the doctor. Jimmy paced the floor waiting for the doctor to emerge from the room. The room door opened and the doctor appeared reassuring him that everything was as it should be, and he should simply let nature take its course. Smiling he took Jimmy's hand, shaking it vigorously, "Congratulations Mr Muirhead, you are going to be a father." As the doctor left he recommended that Jimmy should ensure that Helen got plenty of rest, which was easier said than done. As James thought, Helen was having none of it, and that night she was back at the club putting the young people through their paces.

There had been a big change to the club since the arrival of the Sunbeams and it was becoming apparent that he would need to modify the structure of the club. One change was to the concert party. When the performers had been younger the Sunbeams consisted of both male and female entertainers. But as they got older, it seemed that boys and girls were separated into different activities and roles, not just within the club's structure but in society. The girls tended to be more behind the scenes making costumes, doing makeup and the boys more the performers. Helen had on several occasions suggested to James that, since the girls worked equally hard as the boys; they should be encouraged more to perform. James had gone over and over the idea. It would be going against the structure of society and yet, he felt in his heart that this was the way forward for the youth of today, as long as they were adequately supervised. So it became; boys and girls worked together, performed together but most importantly rehearsed together.

This was a new concept. There were boys' clubs and girls' clubs, but never mixed clubs. Even within the Maryhill Club the boys and girls were divided into two sections, but very soon James realised that his instincts were correct. The boys and girls worked so well together that other activities were included such as hand balancing, the choir and drama group. Dancing soon followed suit and became mixed. However something would not change. This was keep fit because of the natural way their bodies differed.

There was one other change required. That was the need for bigger premises, before they were too cramped and the youths would lose interest. The club had grown so rapidly that they now had three hundred members, and the Muirheads found themselves for the first time having to start a waiting list.

1939
THE WAR

James searched long and hard, but every time new premises were in his reach he was foiled. Either the premises were too small or too costly, but this wasn't his only concern. There was trouble brewing in the continent.

April 1939 and the world was in turmoil. There was talk of war in Europe. Hitler had already invaded Austria and parts of Czechoslovakia. Hitler's youth movement was growing and getting stronger but in 1, Hillside Avenue in Bearsden something special was happening. On the 9th of April, Helen Muirhead gave birth to a son, Robert junior, and for a brief time they could forget the troubles of the world and enjoy their new addition to the family.

The Maryhill Youth Club waiting list was growing as rapidly as the membership and still they had not been able to secure suitable premises.

Helen was finding that juggling family life with the club was proving increasingly difficult. It was Robert senior that stepped in to offer Helen support by looking after Robert junior in the evenings. He was proud of his son's achievements and believed in him.

The club's activities were expanding with a new programme of agilities for both boys and girls, hand balancing as well as a newly formed pipe band, football and boxing. Their club members had outgrown the friendly matches between clubs, and were spreading out into the world of sport where they were becoming skilled in that area. Their reputation was growing within the sporting world. They were becoming aspiring athletes.

The Sunbeams were also increasing in their reputation as performers. They were strictly amateur in the world of entertainment, but their status preceded them as they became like experienced professional entertainers.

Then came the day that Britain was dreading, 1st September when Hitler invaded Poland. On the 3rd September Britain declared war against Germany. The day had finally come which every man, woman and child had feared. It wasn't until the 10th of May 1940 that the clouds of war burst out across the skies of Britain. Every able bodied man and woman was called to war, and in most places in Britain it was the young and elderly who were left behind.

People joined the forces, others went into factories to make ammunition and people joined the A.R.P or the land army. Most women of this time worked in the home. Now the men were going to war, women found themselves the main workforce. Almost every task that had been previously restricted to men was taken over by women, and this was to change attitudes towards women in the work force after the war and for generations to come. But right now this was a nation preparing for war, everyone, young and old, pulled together to do their bit for the war effort and the Maryhill Club was no exception.

James and Helen had secured new premises at 43 Doncaster Street, and not a moment too soon as this war was going to impact on the future development of the Maryhill Club. Two days after war was declared on Hitler, James made significant changes to the club. Firstly he addressed the Sunbeams. They had outgrown their name. They were no longer small Sunday school children, they were young people, so James came up with the name Maryhill Follies. The next and probably the most significant change to the concert party were the performers themselves. He extended his company of entertainers to include their own orchestra while expanding their entertainment programme. These performers may have been amateurs, but they were all shining stars and professional in every aspect of their presentation and performances. Also the club did other things such as making jewellery, soft toys from recycled materials, and wooden toys. They even helped the community make jams and preserves and helped the elderly.

The average age of a Follie was 16 years, the youngest being 14 years old. With serious dedication they performed all over Scotland, entertaining for the British Red Cross, to raise money for food parcels and medical supplies, and they helped raise money for the A.R.P and first aid units. But first and foremost they entertained the people of Maryhill to help keep community spirits high.

The Maryhill Follies

The next few chapters through the war years are dedicated to a special group of youngsters. When talking of war we associate children as victims or refugees, but in Maryhill there was a different type of child. We are talking of youths, whose average age was 16 years, with some being very much younger who became war workers. We knew that youths at 14 years old would be leaving school to start work, and getting married at eighteen. Life was harder. Youths had taken on responsibilities sooner in this era. Not all of us lived in these times but it was still too young to be leaving school and entering the grown up world, never mind as a war worker.

This is a very deserved but small recognition for the members of the Maryhill Youth Club who did their bit for the war. As for the Maryhill Follies, there are probably very few service men and women living who saw them, but they touched the hearts of all that did.

Let us also remember the club members of the Maryhill Youth Club who lost their lives at Dunkirk and Arromanches and other places throughout the war, and the personal losses of brothers, uncles and fathers of the club members and for Helen Muirhead who lost her three brothers at Dunkirk.

1940 - 1941
THE WARWORKERS BEGIN

1940 and James was now 33 years old, and like many other people who took the war seriously he began to prepare his club members.

The Maryhill Follies were out performing and raising money for the Red Cross and other war charities two or three times a week, but within the club he began activities such as mechanics and a cadet force for boys and girls. James began building and developing structures that would help the club members who in the near future would find themselves fighting for their country. 3rd June and glancing through the Evening News, a small article was lurking in one of the back pages, under the heading, **'YOUTH TRAINING'** making these declarations. *'Maryhill Youth Club's activities in connection with pre-service are extensive and the club claims to be the only one in Glasgow and perhaps in a much wider area with a fully formed girls' service cadet corps. Trained in first aid, they are also at present undergoing training to take over as the complete personnel of a rest centre. Another proud claim is that the Maryhill Youth Club is the only club in Glasgow and again perhaps in Scotland with an army cadet corps (under the wing of the 6th H.L.I.).The club also runs an amateur concert party and orchestra and since the outbreak of war the concert party has been giving shows to the troops and military hospitals at the average rate of two a week.'*

Helen in her cadet uniform.

This was the very beginning of the club members' war contributions. James and Helen Muirhead also took up positions to help the war effort as well as running the Maryhill Youth Club. Helen took a volunteer position with the ambulance service as a nurse, and James joined the A.R.P. unit of Bearsden and Dunbarton district. This was for 48 hours a month allowing him time to run the cadet corps. For the next few years he faithfully carried his military identification card No: M485789 which recognised him as the 2nd Lieutenant of the 6th Battalion H.L.I. Cadet Corps. The rest of the year was spent in the preparation for the war and development and expansion of the concert party.

Military Identification Card.

1941

James was giving the same dedication and enthusiasm to his other war duties as he did with the club. On January 26th the Sunday Mail had this headline, '**GLASGOW SOON NOT TO FEAR FIRE BOMBS.**'

'Glasgow will very soon be proof against fire bombs. The great army of fire fighters organised in any city in Britain is at present being recruited on a voluntary basis. Soon men and women in groups of four with steel helmets and brassards will be seen patrolling every district in the city. They are members of a new supplement fire service.

The Hillfoot housing area has been fully organised by chief warden James Muirhead. Wardens must see that every house has a bucket of water and a bucket of sand and all residents are asked to keep sand at their gates. Mr Muirhead has had special sand bags made, suitable for handling when approaching an incendiary bomb. The residents are buying these sand bags and the profit is being put aside for first aid equipment.'

The youngsters of the Maryhill Youth Club were just as energetic and enthusiastic and determined to do their bit for the war. Club members were training hard and working hard. The Evening News soon discovered this and printed this article under the headlines, '**Maryhill Follies.**'

'I am informed that an excellent combination of the boys and girls drawn from the Maryhill boys and girls club are doing good work just now in raising money for war charities. They are at present giving a series of concerts at first aid posts and depots in connection with the ambulance fund of the A.R.P casualty service and have been instrumental in raising quite a large sum of money for this fund.

The 'Maryhill Follies' as they are called carry their own little orchestra with them. This combination is run and produced by Mr James Muirhead who is well known in business circles in town.'

During these war years the armed forces strategically and geographically split Britain into different command sections, and Maryhill fell under what they called the Scottish Command. The Maryhill Follies' growing reputation and recognition soon brought them to the attention of Scottish Command, specifically Major General F.W.L. Bissett, CBE, DSO, MC. Part of his job was taking care of morale within the armed forces.

That wasn't the only attention they were receiving. This time it was from the Scottish Sunday Express with the headlines, **'MEET THE MARYHILL FOLLIES; THEY REHEARSE ON A BUS'** by a woman reporter. And her opening sentence was *'Maybe one evening recently you heard strange sounds coming from a darkened bus trundling out of Glasgow...and wondered.'*

Most of the performers from the Maryhill Follies worked during the days in shops, factories, engineering and ship yards. Seventeen year old Penelope was a manageress of a bakery by day and by night the torch-singer to the Follies. Jackie was another member; he was the original accordion player who composed the Follies opening theme tune 'Hello again.' Now he worked night shifts and could only perform with the Follies once a fortnight. Several of the original members had joined the forces but made it back occasionally, when on leave, to perform.

The Maryhill Follies would arrive at their club room in Doncaster Street, most straight from their work. Helen Muirhead would be waiting with a supply of tea and sandwiches and a pot of soup which was gratefully received. Some of the boys arrived in their overalls with little or no time to stop and wash their oil-stained faces. They would then board their bus, destination unknown, until their arrival. Scottish Command insisted on this as a matter of security. This also meant that, due to this security, there were no records kept of their magnificent performances. I can tell you that once onboard that bus, the performers would do their final preparation for the show. It wasn't uncommon to see a young boy playing the accordion while being accompanied by two female singers or a dancer tapping out her routine in the passageway of the bus. A group of girls would be sitting on the back seats curling their hair and applying their makeup. Someone else would be strumming the guitar.

The destination sometimes would be a lonely moorland where their gay voices would bring cheers to the lads manning the ack-ack batteries or a camp with a 1,000 soldiers joining in the choruses.

Letters of gratitude were coming in. November 24th and the Glasgow Public Health department ambulance yard, based at the Gorbal Baths, wrote words of 'thanks for such a grand show. They have given a valuable service in raising £15 for the Ambulance Fund.'

December 28th and the Bankhead First Aid depot wrote, *'Everyone has remarked on the performance of the concert party, delightful! The concert party should be congratulated.'*

The youngsters from the Maryhill Youth Club took it all in their stride, even when some of the bigger papers began taking an interest in the club's activities.

The Sunday Post 21ˢᵗ December

42

The Sunday Post on the 21st December printed this headline, **'GLASGOW COUPLE COMMAND ARMY OF 700'** and wrote, *'Maryhill Youth Club has given 700 youngsters an interest in life'* was the opening sentence. *'The Maryhill Follies whose age was now between 14yrs and 18yrs have a ten piece orchestra with dancers and singers; the club has a boys' messenger service for the whole of Glasgow area. The boys and girls cadet corps are now receiving training at the club's new camp at Highfield Farm, Newton Mearns at weekends, where they get outdoor training to fit them for the forces.'*

27th December and The People's Journal also had a bit to say, with the headlines, **'THEY CHEER UP THE WAR WORKERS'** and the opening paragraph was,

'One of the most popular concert parties in Glasgow which has a younger personnel than any other similar combination in the city'. The paper reported that the 'follies' engagements for this month alone were twelve with an orchestra of ten consisting of guitars, violins, piano accordions and drums with ten singers and dancers.

James himself had something to add. *'The idea behind the whole organisation including the concert party is service. Our young performers could find no better use for their talents than providing entertainment for those who are engaged in various forms of national work, in addition to raising monies for worthy charitable objectives.'*

The Maryhill Youth Club was proud to claim the position of the most go-ahead club in Scotland. This was one of the many titles given to them from the press, as the club became more and more sought after by the media. These were exciting times for the club and its members, but James Muirhead stayed focused. Since the early days with the church, his vision had been to help the youth, and he was still striving to achieve that goal.

In November the Glasgow Union of Boys Clubs had enrolled the help of James and his club yet again. The sole purpose of the Glasgow Union of Boys Clubs was to promote and support new and existing boys clubs. The union didn't always support James in his theories and considered his approach radical and unorthodox, but James and his club were headline news and were good publicity for the union's new ventures. They wrote to the Maryhill Club thanking them for an excellent show. *'The band was indeed a great help to us and was just what was required to keep the show together and get the youth centre going. I hope you will help us again when we open Patrick Youth Centre in about ten days' time.'*

James knew fine the underlying agenda concerning organisations such as the Glasgow Union of Boys Clubs but he also knew that they needed his help. They were more actively seeking him out for support and advice in dealing with difficult situations, and the Follies were also in high demand for raising monies for these ventures. In fact it had been suggested on several occasions that the Maryhill Youth Club could be used as a training ground for up and coming youth organisations.

James had learned a lot about youth work over the last seven years, and even though he had positive results in his work it was still all too young in years to have a definite impact on the structure of future clubs, but he never turned down a call for help.

The People's Journal 27ᵗʰ December

44

1942
THE WORK CONTINUES

The premises at Doncaster Street had originally been an old mission hall. The ground floor had a reception hall that led off to several smaller rooms including a kitchen and bathroom and downstairs there was a large drill hall. Upstairs there was a large open hallway leading off to several other rooms and every inch of club premises was in use.

James took one of the larger rooms downstairs which adjoined the kitchen facilities, and turned this into a social area for club members, with a small café. Everyone worked so hard, so he provided this safe place for them to relax and socialise in their free time. It was a warm place in which to sit with a few shabby but comfy chairs and a couch or two which were also rather scruffy and battered. James had either begged or borrowed these from someone, but on a cold night this social room with its coal fire was perfect.

James had always believed the only true way to deal with youngsters of any age was contact. There were kids still hanging around the streets whom James had not yet managed to reach and this is what made him open the first youth café of its time. This is when he opened his club doors a little wider, and he offered the youths of Maryhill a place to belong in rather than the streets, hoping that their curiosity would entice them to join the club.

George McMillan was one of these youngsters. "The streets were getting a bit rough even for me and I was a local lad," he said. "I had been ill most of my childhood, having suffered from T.B in 1939. It took a terrible toll on my body leaving me with problems in the joints of my legs. I really fancied joining the boxing team but there was no way, but I did go often to the canteen they opened. It was grand and the other kids who went there were a good bunch," he laughed. "You could get a hot pie, tea and other things to eat, and I seemed to remember that the Girls Cadet Corps ran the canteen and did home baking, and if my memory serves me correctly they weren't bad to look at either!"

He smiled. George is now 82 years old and had many stories to tell, but this one always came to mind when he thought of the Maryhill Club. "One of my pals, Joe was his name. He had joined the Maryhill Club and was in the Army Cadets. One night, on the way to Doncaster Street, Joe and me stopped at an ice-cream shop, on Trossachs Street. Trossachs Street used to be quiet, but lately there had been trouble with a gang running around in those long macs, you know the type Colombo used to wear. Anyway this gang were carrying knives around and frightening the hell out of everyone. We went in to the ice-cream shop, and the moment we entered it went silent. My mum had got given a mac and she thought I could get some use from it. Even though she had sewn it to make it fit it was still too big for me. Anyway, we were in this ice cream shop.

There was four men standing who were talking to the owner, and now they were all staring at me. My pal Joe realised that something was up and hurried me out of the shop. I stopped outside to ask Joe what was up, when these four men came out the door after us shouting the odds. One of the men grabbed me and pushed me hard against the wall and shouted, "Where all your hard men pals now mate?" I was so scared I couldn't utter a word. I was surrounded by these big burly men all shouting at once. Then over the top of their voices I began to hear a rumble. It was the sound of tacky boots on the run, then there was deadly silence. Instantly the man released his grip and the others stopped shouting. That's when I saw Joe and about twenty of his mates all in their cadet uniforms, the men just turned and walked away. The cadets hadn't uttered a single word, they had just stood there with their arms crossed, looking very macho." George laughed, "That was the last time I wore that bloody coat. As I said, the kids from the Maryhill Club, good bunch, they certainly saved my bacon that night."

Unfortunately George's health never improved enough to be an active member of the club, and yet the Muirheads never closed the door on him. He stayed with the club until 1951 when he got married to Jessie Gillespie, (who also for a time was a club member), and they moved to Kings Lynn to work for Campbells Soups.

The Girls Service Corps not only ran the canteen at Doncaster Street, but gave various displays with their first aid and showed off their rifle skills. On the 5th June the Evening Times reminded us of this, with the headline, '**MARYHILL YOUTH SCHEME IN ACTION**' telling us all of the forthcoming display on the 10th June by the Girls Service Cadets at Doncaster Street.

The Boys Army Cadets, (the Cameroonians as they were called), were working alongside the Home Guard as well as running a messenger service and giving displays. The 6th Battalion Highland Light Infantry Cadet Corps sent their congratulations in a letter dated 19th June that year, stating that their work was splendid and *'the success of the unit would benefit hundreds of young men in the Maryhill area.'* Also the Glasgow Union of Boys Clubs expressed their thanks for the army cadets services on the 22nd June.

The concert party was working harder than ever, with up to three engagements a week, under the guidance of Scottish Command, and there were performances for different organisations on top of their other commitments. The military hospital at Gilshochill, Glasgow, expressed their patients' delight at the marvellous entertainment from the Maryhill Follies. On the 22nd October there was another letter of thanks, this time from the British Red Cross Parcels for Prisoners of War fund, for yet another marvellous concert to help with their funds.

Letters of thanks kept pouring in and so did the letters asking for help from the club. The club members just kept on working; they did not falter in their enthusiasm or their ability to serve others.

The Maryhill Youth Club wasn't all work and no play. During the week the club ran arts and crafts, gymnastics, wood working classes and a pipe band among their many activities.

However, on a Sunday night, they would have a concert party show and use of the canteen, exclusively for club members only, with a dance once a month for those who had attended their activities regularly. There was one other thing that the Club members did. They ran one night a month for the parents and friends who helped the Maryhill Club, with everyone working so hard. Parents had come forward to help with making of scenery or obtaining props or giving material to help with costumes, some even made costumes, others helped out with supplies of wood. So as a thank you the Maryhill Club ran a social evening of bingo, or maybe a bridge night, and occasionally a dance which they used as a fund raising event.

1943
THE VALLEY GANG

The churches weren't successful at bringing youths through the church doors, and were becoming quite alarmed at the rise in gang activities. Even the police and council officials were at a loss as how to control these youths.

James however had other ideas. He suggested to the churches and other youth-oriented organisations that a policy of 'open doors' could work for them, a place that ran seven days a week, where these youths could function on a daily basis, in a safer environment, by putting their spare time and energies into something positive that they could help create. He explained the benefits which his own club members were getting from 'open doors' policy. The churches were appalled at the suggestion of Sunday opening for anything other than religious reasons. No-one was prepared to stand out from the crowd and go against the church's view, especially on this shaky territory, no-one except for James.

The papers this year weren't only reporting on the war but also on the increasing number of youths who were becoming harder to control. There had been talk in the paper for sometime about the 'Manchester Project', a youth facility which had been set up as an experimental project to help combat the problem of gangs, and the youths that were spiralling out of control. The project had failed drastically. Instead of tackling the problem it increased the issues by giving them a place to play snooker, listen to music, a place to spiral out of control in.

James had been working with the youth in Doncaster Street for nearly four years now, and he had his fair share of dealing with the local gangs in the past. James had been actively making contact with gang members in a bid to recruit them into the Maryhill Youth Club, and on some levels he had succeeded in bringing some gang members into the fold of the club.

The gang problem was growing fast. Some of these gangs were becoming quite powerful by their presence as well as their activities. People were more aware of the public lack of ability to resolve this issue and they were scared. Even the police were unable to control these youths and the situations these gangs were creating were escalating into unbearable conditions. The Bulletin printed this headline, '**ONLY GANG MEMBERS ELIGIBLE.**' *'Members of a Glasgow gang which have been noted for their activities for sometime in gang warfare and other exploits will be the only people eligible for membership of a new youth club to be opened soon in Glasgow.'* The papers also reported that a well known youth leader wanted to set up a facility for gangs on condition they ceased all gang activities. It was also suggested that a meeting was being held between this youth leader and official members of the Boys Union and Girls Union of Clubs to discuss this matter. The paper had to say about this particular gang. *'This gang has a membership of a hundred youths whose age is 16 to 20 years. They will be given the chance of recreation and physical exercise, boxing, football and gymnastics as well as other pursuits within the club.'*

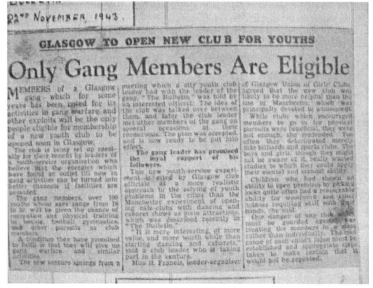

Story printed by The Bulletin

When these reports reached the ears of this particular gang, they started a course of intimidation towards James and Helen Muirhead and the members of the Maryhill Youth Club. Some time passed and they realised that their approach wasn't having the desired effect, so the Valley Gang sent the Muirheads a sympathy card in the September of 1943. The words *'With loving sympathy'* greeted James and Helen on the outside of the card and printed inside was *'Please accept our sincere sympathy'* with the hand written words, *'For by God you'll need it.'* The word on the street was the Valley Gang were after the Muirheads. The police suggested that James and Helen should shut up shop to defuse the situation, but they weren't going to be bullied into anything.

The sympathy card

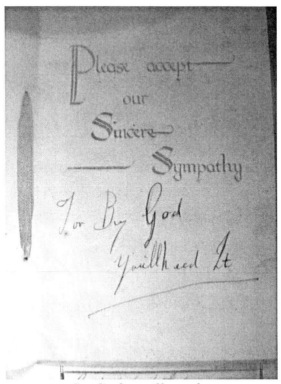

By God you'll need it

The Maryhill Club continued as normal. Club members travelled in groups and for a while all was quiet. Then one evening as club members were training hard, the police arrived. The Muirheads ushered them into the staffroom. The sergeant was extremely anxious. It had come to his attention that the Valley Gang were on the move and it's suspected destination was Doncaster Street. The police begged the Muirheads to send their members home as they could not ensure anyone's safety.

James and Helen had other ideas. They sent the members home except for their army cadets. The Muirheads deployed the cadets armed with their rifles, empty of course, into the surrounding buildings to hide. Then James and Helen stood out side and waited. They didn't have long to wait.

The gang arrived, knuckle dusters and all. James tried to reason with the leaders. These young men were angry, they wanted action not talk; they were on a mission to take out that interfering goody two shoes, Jimmy Muirhead, once and for all. James was surrounded. They weren't interested in Helen. They just wanted to teach James a good lesson. Helen acted quickly. She knew fine well that the only way to resolve this situation was to play them at their own game. She took the whistle which was always hung around her neck and blew it hard. The cadets stepped out from the nearby buildings with their rifles aimed. The gang was surrounded. There was nowhere to run. All they could do was to throw down their weapons in defeat. James and the gang entered into, shall we say, negotiations? They were agreed and it was decided that James would set up a club for them and them alone. But there was to be one condition; James insisted they would have to stop all gang ventures; any members found breaking this agreement would be out on their ears. And true to their word, the Muirheads opened an annex for the gang members only and the gang stopped their ventures. Never at anytime did James consider that a separate club would be a permanent arrangement, he only viewed it as a stepping stone, as a means to integrate these youths into the main structure club.

Unfortunately for James, he found himself once more out on a limb. Every time he went forward with a new approach in youth work, he found himself standing alone with only his wife's support. The other official bodies in youth work gave him their problems to resolve, then they stood well back to watch him fail. His approach to youths was different. It was radical, well before his time, and he always put his money where his mouth was. He led from the front. Often James would say, "This is what we should do" and while others debated the pros and cons, meeting after meeting, James was out there doing it, with positive results.

In the October of this year, the Evening News printed an article. The headline was '**BOYS' CLUBS.'** It reported that thirty eight clubs were affiliated with the Glasgow Union of

Boys Clubs. They were holding their A.G.M. and there would be much debate on the state of juveniles the following week.

'The Lord Provost and General Sir Andrew Thorne of Scottish Command will be among the speakers.' "I don't think any of the speakers will touch on the subject of juvenile delinquency. The idea of these boys clubs is not to cure juvenile delinquency but to prevent it."'

The city was concerned and pressuring officials, who were now gathering to deal with the issue of youths, but James Muirhead was convinced that until they learned to talk the talk and walk the walk they would fail.

James tackled each issue as it happened in his life, but nothing seemed to interfere with the running of the club. Through this difficult period, the Maryhill Youth Club had been preparing for yet another display from its talented members. Tickets were being sent to parents and friends of the club for a Musical Review which would include dancing, piping, acrobatics and gymnastics and was to be held on Tuesday the 2nd November.

The ticket

1943
LETTERS IN THE POST

Helen's mornings comprised of house work, making breakfast and setting the fire in their small sitting room. By 10 am she was settling down with James for morning tea before spending until lunch time reading and answering the daily correspondence. Most of the letters comprised of booked performances of the Follies or booking displays for other groups who worked with youth development, and lots of letters of thanks and appreciation.

The Glasgow Union of Girls Clubs was frequently in the Muirheads' mail, with words of encouragement. They were desperately trying to develop and support the involvement of girls within clubs.

Unfortunately some of the parents weren't quite as supportive as James and Helen would have liked. They genuinely believed that the club contributed to these young people's lives. Some of the youths they worked with came from socially upstanding backgrounds; others came from poor and tough backgrounds, but the club was there to help all, especially those who needed it the most, to have confidence with a positive outlook to life. They would not be made to choose which youths to help, and some parents had shown their disgust at their children mixing with disadvantaged youths.

Now that the gang members were playing a part in the club meant that their friends and girlfriends also came. Some of the parents had gone to the point of withdrawing their children.

Shuffling through these letters Helen noticed one addressed to herself. She began opening it curiously, after all it wasn't often she got personal mail.

'26.10.43
Dear Mrs Muirhead,

    I was wondering if you would consider taking Nancy back to the club. I have realized what I have done keeping her away from it.

    There is nothing wrong with the club and the girls are decent, and respectable. I now take back all that I said about the club and the girls.

    Yours faithfully,
    E Grant'

Smiling, Helen placed the letter on the reply pile. James was opening yet another letter. He replaced his letter opener on the coffee table, and surveying the contents he shook his head. "Helen, I think you should read this," he said as he handed Helen the letter, his expression grim. Helen began to read:-

'7 Ashcroft Street
 Glasgow

26.10.43
Dear Mr and Mrs Muirhead

    I am sorry for all the trouble and worries I have brought upon you. I'm sorry I didn't make the grade, but I have learned that you can't have your pie and eat it. Please don't try and communicate with me, it would help things a lot if you would just forget the boy named James Little. The boy that tried to make good but failed in every sense of the word. I have found happiness in the club, a happiness I didn't deserve. There is just one more thing; I want you both to remember just one thing of me. Wherever I go whatever I do in my life time, I will always remember the two finest people in the world are Mr and Mrs Muirhead.

    Your greatest admirer,
    Jimmie'

Helen put the letter down and spoke, "James, this is wrong. He hasn't brought anything on us. We knew fine well what could happen with kids like Jimmie. He thinks he is no good but he's wrong, we have failed him."

James rested a reassuring hand on Helen. "We have only failed him if we do nothing," he said.

Working with these youths had been difficult, it wasn't easy for them to change the habits they had always known. Sometimes these youths got into trouble, not because they were still doing wrong, but because of their history of associated gang crimes, and Jimmie Little was one of these youths. He had been a member of the Valley Gang eighteen months ago. James had influenced Jimmie enough to join the club. At first Jimmie would sneak into the club afraid of what his gang friends might do to him if they found out. James wondered, now that the whole Valley Gang was here, whether things would be difficult for Jimmie. The Muirheads went to see Jimmie and it wasn't long before he returned to the club. Unfortunately Jimmie became a bombardier and lost his life for his country like so many good people before and after him.

The war was taking its toll on the Maryhill Club. James had seen a lot of the young club members join the forces or take up their war duties. Most of the Valley Gang had joined the Cadet Corps and moved shortly after into the services and many of them took part in the D Day landings in Normandy.

James always found it hard to hear about the death of a club member, even though he was grateful to the grieving parents for keeping him informed, but sometimes the news wasn't all bad.

One night a young man was far away from his friends and family. Like so many others, getting news from home kept his spirits high. He hoped that the war would soon be over and he could go back to his life as he knew it. Eddie Laughlin was sitting in his barracks. He was with the 10th Battalion H.L.I. He had seen several articles in the Glasgow papers mentioning the Maryhill Youth Club and putting pen to paper he wrote to

James. Eddie had been an original member of the club when it was in Garscube Road. He was the goalkeeper in the Woodside Boys Club football team, and was hoping after the war he could come back to the club. Eddie finished with these lovely words, *"You are doing a great job Mr Muirhead. Keep it up for Glasgow's all."*

There was something special about this club. Once you became a member, your loyalties were strong. These youngsters were growing into adults and most of them were staying with the club and those who had left were waiting eagerly to return.

1944
PIONERING PROGRESS

James was beginning to achieve his goals and fulfilling his dreams. His vision had been to reach out to all the youths of Maryhill, and the results were excellent. In a decade of tried and tested methods, there had been some hiccups along the way and always there would be lessons to learn. His theories in working with the youths of that time were so good, James was branching out with his skills and experience into teaching techniques in youth work and development. He was travelling around the countryside, meeting with officials who were setting up new club ventures or going to other clubs as an adviser. The club rooms in Doncaster Street were also becoming a meeting and training ground for officials of other clubs seeking advice or just sampling some of the wonderful activities of the Maryhill Club. There were also other clubs visiting for friendly matches of football and boxing as well as competitive tournaments that would take place there.

One of these visits was from two officers of the Army Cadet Corps headquarters, who had come to inspect the club's Cadets Corps, the Cameroonians. One officer was so surprised by what he encountered that he put pen to paper and wrote,

'Dear Mr Muirhead,

We were so impressed, when we visited you on Monday night, by the splendid work you are doing in Maryhill. I do not refer entirely to the question of the cadet training, but to your activities as a whole, which, most apparently, are bearing excellent results.

The enthusiasm shown by everyone demonstrates what can be done by a movement such as yours. Such work is bound to make itself felt, and must influence the standard of life in the district.'

James had always said the motto of the club was to serve others, and he was not kidding. Every activity in the club gave performances or demonstrations; every member had a goal to achieve, a sense of belonging, a sense of pride but mostly a sense of purpose.

The Pipe Band

The club was always preparing for concerts. One of these was in the Woodside Public Halls. The Evening Times on the 21st of September ran a small article, to remind us of the event with the title, **'MARYHILL FOLLIES PERFORM.'** *'Maryhill Follies at the Woodside Hall, will be supported by the club's own pipe band.'* The reporter was obviously a fan of the Follies stating, *'I have seen them on many occasions.'* Even the Daily Record announced on the 22nd September of the up and coming performance under the heading, **'THRIVING YOUTH CLUB.'**

A common venue for the club's concerts was at the St Andrew's Halls in Glasgow.

The Glasgow Herald printed this on the 9th November, under the heading, **'PROGRESS OF YOUTH IN ACTION.'**

'Display in St Andrew's Halls on the 14th November will be the high water mark for the year in the activities of a city club, which was a pioneer in youth welfare and is still a model for later ventures to follow. A feature of the club is that the children run it themselves to a large extent under the supervision of James and Helen Muirhead. As a tribute to the club's service in entertaining the forces, Major-general F. W. L. Bissett will preside at the display'.

There were always other groups and clubs around all eager to help solve the increasing problems that youths were experiencing. Many of them were rigid in their thought and approach, others just didn't get to the heart of the matter or couldn't reach out to the youngsters.

There was however another club in the area which was making significant progress. This club, which was associated with Burnbank Church of Scotland, was run by the Rev. W. N. Scott with the assistance of the Police Inspector J. Mclellan.

The club had a hundred members and offered swimming, a canteen and Saturday night lectures from local celebrities. They also had a Sunday night service, after which there was a group discussion. The Sunday Post ran a small article with the heading, **'LUCKY YOUTHS'** stating, *'The two most enterprising clubs in Glasgow are in the North West, the Burnbank Church and the Maryhill Youth Club.'*

The Maryhill Youth Club was definitely not the only club in Glasgow, but they had something that was working, as they never had less than three hundred members and an ever growing list of activities.

The Bulletin ran a large feature on the Maryhill Club on the 9th November with the heading, **'CLUB CHANGED A SLUM DISTRICT.'** *'It's the kind of street the police used to keep their eye on. Grey blocks of tenements shut out the sky. There was nowhere for the children to play but in the roadway and the closes, and someone was always complaining about the noise and the rowdiness. Broken windows were not infrequent and gangs of youngsters created wild scenes in the street, in fact* *it was just the kind of place where juvenile delinquents might grow into something worse. That was Doncaster Street and its environs before the Maryhill Youth Club.'* This was the first paragraph of the article, before the reporter launched into the story of the beginnings of the club. After that publication, the Bulletin office began receiving donations for the Maryhill Youth Club from members of the public.

George Outram & Co. was the publisher of the Bulletin and sent the grand sum of £30.00, together with this letter from one anonymous member of the public, which was addressed to the editor of the Bulletin.

The Bulletin

'Dear Sirs,

In the Bulletin, Thursday 9th of November there was an article on a youth club run by Mr Muirhead and his wife. I think such a club deserves the advertisement you gave and also your support, as well as outside support. I have enclosed a £5.00 donation for this club. I will not give my name but I will make a stipulation that you put a paragraph in the Bulletin that you have received this money. It may entice others who read it to do the same and send a donation along and every little bit helps.'

James sent a letter to the Bulletin, thanking all those who had sent donations, for the only times the club received regular donations were still through their annual displays.

14th November and the concert at the St Andrew's Halls had been a great success. They also managed to celebrate a little as this was their tenth annual display.

A hundred club members, both boys and girls, took part in this display and performed to an audience of nearly eight hundred. The programme was a variety of entertainment by the concert party, physical fitness and exercise by junior and senior members. The outstanding musical performance was from the club's pipe band, which was for the first time rendering in public a composition called Captain Muirhead. This was composed by the pipe major of the band Donald Mctaggert in honour of their club leader, James Muirhead.

The Bulletin on the 15th November held the heading, **'YOUTH CLUB'S WORK PRAISED'** and the Glasgow Herald's heading was, **'YOUTH DISPLAY IN GLASGOW, CLUB'S ACHIEVEMENT.'** Both papers reported this,

'Major-General Bissett complimented the club's leader James Muirhead and the young people who took part in the display on their high standard of achievement and strong evidence of team spirit.' Then he said, *"Such clubs as yours are absolutely essential. Their provision all over the country should go hand in hand with legislation for social security, housing, health and education."* He finished with special thanks from the forces for

the concerts which the club's concert party had given over the previous four years.

James never charged anyone who needed the Maryhill Club to perform. Sometimes there was a donation for fuel so it was nice when people gave donations.

Mr. Jaconelli, confectioner and tobacconist at 570 Maryhill Road, sent James and Helen a letter with a donation of 10/- (50p) with warm words *'for your club which is doing a marvellous job in these difficult times.'*

The Ministry of Labour and National Service sent their letter of thanks on the wonderful display at St. Andrew's Halls.
Major-General Bissett also sent his letter of thanks with a donation of £25 from his *'own private funds.'*

The Maryhill Follies also received a letter from Scottish Command, wishing them to attend a tribute in the form of a social dance for all voluntary artists who had entertained the troops untiringly. *'All artists who have performed more than twenty five performances will receive a badge and certificate for their hard work during the war years.'* This function would be held in the May of 1945.

1945
THE WAR ENDS BUT THE CLUB STILL ADVANCES

In 1938 James and Helen had begun to integrate boys and girls working together, firstly in the concert party and then into other activities. The Union of Boys Clubs and the Union of Girls Clubs were not supportive of this particular idea. They had concluded that James was overstepping the boundaries regarding the sexes and the churches were in agreement. They felt strongly that the youths' morals were in danger.

James was always breaking new ground in his advancing approach to youth work. The Maryhill Youth Club was the first of its kind and sadly there has been nothing quite like it since.

The Evening Times however was sympathetic towards James; or rather they knew there was always news with the Maryhill Club. The Evening Times had a weekly column called 'Scottish Youth Home Front' which they wrote under the heading, '**MIXED CLUB A SUCCESS**.'

'Club leaders who draw a rigid line between the activities of lads and girls might with profit spend an evening at that virile organisation the Maryhill Youth Club. This mixed club has all the usual units, but in addition encourages the sexes to take an interest in the work of each other.'

James didn't worry too much about other people's reactions. It certainly wasn't pleasant listening to how people viewed his moral standing or that his ideas were creating so much negativity. He just knew that they were working, as was his table tennis team. This had been a new venture for the club, which had been influenced by the Americans during the war. Table tennis was the latest craze and they were now taking part in a local league that had been set up by the Glasgow Union of Boys Clubs.

They had just played the Hutchesontown Boys Club with good results, and the club leader, Thomas Lamb, wrote these words, *'Maryhill boys are the greatest bunch of fellows, with the familiarity of a friend. I congratulate you on having boys who are a credit to you and their club. We at our club are wishing you continued success in your great work, amongst the Maryhill boys.'*

The British Broadcasting Corporation were very interested in the club and sent a letter on the 27th January after reading an article about the Follies in the Bulletin.

'I am interested in the prospects of doing a short broadcast about the club's activities, say in one of our Scottish half hour programmes. You will understand, of course, that at the moment the idea is only a mere project and will depend on how much broadcasting material we find.'

James was delighted and eagerly agreed for the broadcasting company to visit the club at Doncaster Street, this being on top of the club's very busy schedule.

1st March and the Maryhill Follies were in concert again only this time to raise money for the local Sea Cadet Corps to keep the unit running. The Clydebank press wrote, **'Successful concert by the Maryhill Follies.'** *'They provided a fine show in the town hall'.*

The original poster

The Maryhill Follies were rehearsing for their forthcoming performance. The poster read,

MARYHILL YOUTH CLUB
Present their
FORCES' FAVOURITE CONCERT PARTY

MARYHILL FOLLIES
With their swing band
PIPE BAND AND GIRLS SERVICE CADETS

In the
LYRIC THEATRE
FRIDAY, 3rd AND SATURDAY 4th MARCH 7.30 p.m.
STALLS 2/6 2/-   CIRCLE 3/- 2/-   GALLERY 1/-

The Maryhill Club members for the last two years had performed a play annually and this year was no different. On the 20th March they performed at the Lyric Theatre a short play entitled 'Evening Times,' a comedy take on the paper, with musical entertainment from the Maryhill Follies.

The British Broadcasting Company had been several times to visit, and were so delighted with the Maryhill Club that they decided to broadcast. 21st March and the Radio Times read, *'Wednesday General Forces programme 5.00 Scottish Half-hour introduces a concert by the BBC Scottish Orchestra and a recorded visit to a Glasgow youth club.'*

24th March and the Maryhill boxing team made the Evening News. *'Maryhill Youth Club winners of the City Businessmen's Boxing Shield. Team members are J.Thomson, E.Winters, W.M'Cann, J.Darrack, W.M'Cabe, E.Blanche, D.Dougan, W.Brice, J.Birkins, R.Danks, and R.Baird. A move is on hand to match these boys with the winners of the London's Boys Federation tournament.'*

James and Helen Muirhead had now taken on a secretary to deal with the ever increasing number of letters and replies. One of these letters stood out. It was from a young service man, Bill Paul who was with the R.A.F.

The Boxing team

'*Dear Mr Muirhead,*

I have only time for a few lines, but I thought I must write to congratulate you, Mrs Muirhead, and the members of the club, who took part in the broadcast in 'Scottish Half-hour.' It did me the world of good to sit and listen here in Belgium to what was going on in 'the club', while I was waiting on orders 'to move'.

I sat in the billet writing a letter when another Jock switched on the wireless and said to me, 'Hey Jock stop writing just now, Scottish Half-hour will be on in a couple of minutes'

When I heard it announced that they were broadcasting a recording from a club in Scotland, I knew at once there was only one club worthy of that and that's Maryhill Youth Club. The band went over a treat. My heart swelled with pride to think I was once a member of that band which has reached the stage of broadcasting through the B.B.C.

Well Mr Muirhead I am afraid that is all I have time for just now, so until it's all over.
All the best,
Bill'

Even during these hard times, the Maryhill Club gave out a sense of belonging and pride, of being part of something special, and was always close to the hearts of those who had been part of it.

The village of Caldwell had decided to tackle their youth problems in the form of a youth club and they enrolled the services of the Maryhill Youth Club. James was only too eager to help Caldwell with its development. The Torrance Youth Club, as it was to be called, would celebrate its opening night with a concert from the Maryhill Follies and the Maryhill Youth Club did it in style. The event was spectacular, starting the celebrations with the Maryhill Pipe Band leading a procession of both clubs through the village, before the start of the evening concert.

The Maryhill Follies delighted its audience rendering songs old and new including Scots, Irish, Western and Negro numbers, (which was the term used in those days), together with popular dances.

2nd May and a letter from Scottish Command with invites to the social evening for the Maryhill Follies and congratulations for the badges and certificates they were to receive for all their hard work.

1st June and the Maryhill Pipe Band accompanied by the Maryhill Girls Service Cadets hit the streets to raise money for the Wings of Victory and raised a grand total of £8.00.

8th June and the Maryhill Club's Army Cadet Corps had grown rapidly. They were now recognised by the British National Cadet Association.

The war was finally over and the Maryhill Follies and other members of Maryhill Youth Club had raised a lot of money for the war effort and had given over a thousand voluntary concerts to the troops but they found themselves in just as much demand.

Lady Lithgow was now chairwoman of the Association of Girls Clubs and had earlier that year enrolled the help of the Maryhill Youth Club to put on an inter-club display at the St Andrew's Halls. This was quite an event. It involved all the girls clubs who were affiliated to the Union of Girls Clubs in the one hall doing various activities. James willingly took the challenge of organising the sequence of events. Lady Lithgow was so impressed by James' leadership skills, as well as his natural organisational skills, she began to frequent the Maryhill Youth Club as an observer. She was delighted to be the guest of honour at the club's annual display, which was held this time in the Lyric Theatre on the 28th September. The annual show was a sensation with a full house at the theatre. Lady Lithgow was so pleased she sent James a letter of thanks stating,

'I have much pleasure in enclosing a cheque for £25.00. This contribution comes from me simply as a friend of the club not as chairman of the association.'

James had been asked to give a talk at the St Andrew's Men's Club, the topic being 'Religion and Youth Work.' The other main speaker was the Rev. A. Bowyers. James accepted the invitation. Those who were to attend the talk would not be prepared for his forward views on youth work or the passion and drive he had for his club. They were about to discover this wasn't just his work, this was his life.

The Bellshill speaker was delighted to report on the 2nd November the discussion at the St Andrew's Men's Club.

'Mr Muirhead gave a stirring address on the work among the youths especially in the Maryhill District. His remarks on his relations with organised religion were controversial but friendly.

James, who had faced the tough youth of Maryhill, considered if you left religion out of it no matter how tough they were or thought they were you could do something with them.' The reporter added this, *'After visiting the Maryhill Youth Club I can*

vouch for its success. The youth of Maryhill trust Mr Muirhead completely because they know he has no other fish to fry and that he has no political end. His only payment is his pride at their success.'

James also spent a lot of time sending letters to companies in Glasgow. In November of that year he sent letters to the City Bakeries in St Georges Square and Change Brothers Limited in Firhill offering the facilities of the Maryhill Youth Club to the young apprentices and young girls of their companies. James had even made a brochure for this purpose; here are some of its contents.

'Maryhill Youth Club
Aims. 1. To provide a centre of comradeship for boys and girls in the district.
(Primarily between the ages of 14 and 19 years).
2. To encourage all members to cultivate their moral and physical well being.

The Activities of the club include:

Lads	*Girls*
Physical training	*Physical training*
Boxing	*Hockey*
Football	*Motor Mechanics*
Miniature rifle club	*Miniature rifle club*
Motor mechanics	*First aid*
First aid	*Cookery*
Discussion groups	*Sick nursing*
Concert party	*Concert party*
Pipe band	*Pipe band*
Army cadets' unit	*Girls' service cadets*

This club is open each evening (Sundays included) from 7 to 10.30, has a games room, a lounge and a canteen.'

71

Christmas was fast approaching and the Maryhill Club was preparing for some hard work the week before Christmas. During that week in their club rooms at Doncaster Street for three consecutive nights, the drama group would be presenting three one act plays. On the Friday evening there would be a display of articles made by the boys' and girls' arts and crafts and the boys' wood work and engineering classes.

James was now going to discover the effects of the war on the Maryhill Club. The club was going to be strongly influenced by their work with both British and American forces. The end of the war was going to bring so many changes that the club would soon be running 14 hours a day seven days a week.

1946
SOMETHING OLD, SOMETHING NEW

The war had left many influences in Britain such as tinned jams and meats and of course nylon stockings brought in by the American forces. James and the club had spent a lot of time over the last few years with the forces both British and American. He had often seen the American soldiers playing basketball and it was a game that intrigued him. In fact he was so taken with the game that by 1944 he had started his own basketball team, playing friendly games with the soldiers, and the Americans were only too happy to teach the Maryhill Youth Club the game.

Extract 'The Glasgow Herald'

James wasn't the only one to be influenced by the war, Helen was also developing ideas. In the 1800s when Britain occupied India, the soldiers there learned the art of Indian club and took it on board as a training programme. It was a mixture of juggling and exercise and was very good in the development of upper body strength. Through time it filtered through all of the forces. The Air Force also had India clubs which they swung keeping their arms straight, and was used for exercise purposes. This had similar movements and actions as the flag waving for the aeroplanes.

This was what Helen had seen and it inspired her. Getting herself a set of Indian clubs, she found that they were exceptionally heavy, as they were filled with sand. After a lot of perseverance she began to conquer the clubs and began developing a style of swinging that suited the female frame. Soon Helen discovered that if she bent her arms she could swing these clubs in an elegant manner, combined with some grace and exercise movements already used in the girls' keep fit classes. She was sure that she had a winner. Quickly she put together a routine. James was so impressed by the club swinging that he agreed to a trial period. Helen selected six girls and trained them. Three months later every girl in the club wanted to be in the India club team. This was a sight to behold, twenty girls on the floor in four lines of five, all swinging their clubs, and moving up and down the hall in perfect sequence, and, trust me, it needed to be. Helen taught me to swing these Indian clubs which weren't easily mastered, but after a few black eyes and the occasional sore chin, usually because I wasn't quick enough or was just in the wrong place at the wrong time, the training paid off with success. It was also an honour to have been part of something so special and unique the like of which had never been seen before and will probably never be seen again.

Indian Club Team

There was still work to be done. The Knightswood Youth Club needed funds and had requested a performance of the Maryhill Concert Party.

For years now the churches had been up in arms about the open doors policy that clubs like the Maryhill used. The churches felt strongly that these clubs should not be open on a Sunday. James, a long time ago had tried to persuade his church to have the policy of open doors. Something new had emerged and this angered the churches more, Sunday entertainment. This was a day of worship, there should only be evenings of Bible studies, or interesting religious accomplishments. Now things had changed, and were still changing.

2nd February and the Evening News had this headline: -
'OPEN DOORS'

Sunday 'open doors' seem fated to remain in the news. Glasgow presbytery's experiment in the Ca'rdoro has now roused interest in Holland and India.

The churches were now supporting 'open doors' launched by the Rev James Connell. Under his watchful eye the scheme was launched even though some ministers still questioned its values.' The reporter for this article had done his homework and told his readers that the *'originator of the 'open door' was no other than James Muirhead of the model Maryhill Club who had for several years now run an open door policy'.*

The Maryhill Club members were as active as ever. On 3rd May they took part in a successful concert for the newly formed Knightswood Central Youth Club for club funds. With help and advice from James, the club was developing its own agenda of summer activities including camping, day outings and omnibus tours.

18th May at Firhill Park there was a football match between the Maryhill Youth Club and the Lanarkshire Select with all the proceeds going to the Scottish Association of Boys Clubs national appeal.

The club also had a league football team, with excellent players and it won many leagues. 18th May and the Maryhill football team was preparing to play a league match against Darvel football club on the Tuesday.

The war was over at last, families and loved ones were being reunited. It was a time of joy, but for some a time of sadness for the loved ones who would not be coming home. The Maryhill Youth Club was no different. It was a time of sadness for those who had died but a time of rejoicing as club members returned from the war and back to the folds of the club. There was a particular club member who returned with a very special gift for the Muirheads.

One young man found himself in Holland at the end of the war. Waiting to be returned home with his unit, he came across six young Dutch girls who had stowed away on the ship which was taking him home. The only things they had in their possession were tulip bulbs, which he believed the girls had been eating. The young soldier could not leave them, so after a few words to his commanding officer, all was agreed. He brought them to James and Helen Muirhead.

These young girls came with only the clothes they wore. The Muirheads did what was natural to them and opened their doors and their hearts and gave the girls a home, until they were eventually returned to their country.

Dutch girls try the bagpipes at a party given in their honour by the Maryhill Youth Club, Glasgow.

Extract Evening Times

After the war N.A.T.O was established and from this came an alliance, also an official body had been formed called World Friendship Association. This was an educational programme to teach the younger generation to build a better world and a better future, hopefully one of peace. Since the Muirheads had already been of great assistance with the Dutch girls, the association contacted James and Helen and on the 30th

August twenty five Dutch girls arrived, hosted by the Maryhill Youth Club.

The Evening Times published some photographs of the girls and their discovery of the bagpipes. The Maryhill Girls Pipe Band loaned the Dutch girls their kilts for a visit to the Cowal games. They received a tour of Edinburgh Castle, the five lochs, and of course no trip would be complete without a trip Doon the Watter to good auld Rothesay on the Isle of Bute. James had been delighted with the visit even though not one of them spoke any English. He was eagerly awaiting next spring because as a thank you, the girls planted bulbs in his garden, Dutch fashion.

Extract Evening Times

July and Lord Rotherwick gave permission to the Newmills British Legion Club to hold a concert in his garden grounds. The Maryhill Youth Club gave their services with pipe music, singing and dancing. There was a large crowd in attendance and £27 was raised at the gates alone. All the money went to the Scottish Veterans Garden's City Association.

September and the Maryhill Youth Club was on hand to help. This time it was the Kirk Lanes Lads Club who had opened new premises and what better way to celebrate its opening than with a concert from the Maryhill Follies. After which the club members began their final preparation for yet another annual display on 16th October in St Andrew's Halls.

The Pathfinder monthly magazine was there to see this performance. In November they had this to say, *'A very high standard of efficiency was shown, through the entire extensive performance which was of a non stop order from start to finish. Youth clubs in the making had much to learn from this display.'*

The Maryhill Basketball Team played the Union Sportive do Point Lévesque, on the 17th October at St Andrew's Hall and lost gracefully to their French opponents.

1st-7th November. This was the week that the Maryhill Club ran their pantomime at Doncaster Street and it also caught the attention of The Pathfinder. Their December issue made this comment. *'Mr J. Muirhead, the club leader, was responsible for the script and production, which was effected on the usual Maryhill Y.C nonstop lines. The cast, which was well chosen and enthusiastic, balanced any evidence of unfinished performance due to lack of experience. This incredible adventure included a real waterfall scène. Carry on Maryhill. What next?'*

Christmas was fast approaching. Last year the club had planned a Christmas party, a meal for the club members and their families. This year they had decided to have a Christmas lunch for the elderly as well. Everyone was looking forward to the event which was to be steak pie and chips. I was informed this was a special treat to be had, and by the looks of things they were going to need it.

There was to be little rest for the club. Already the British Legion had written asking for help to raise £169, this time for another charity they were helping. Others were writing to the Muirheads for their help and support. Next year's calendar was filling up fast.

Extract The Bulletin

1947
A LITTLE REST

'A little rest' was maybe not quite what it would suggest, but this year was one of concentration. James had shown an interest in basketball since 1944 and by 1946 there were junior and senior sections of both male and female basketball teams of the Maryhill Club training and playing. This was something that caught the attention of the young people of Glasgow. With the influx of American service personnel, James quickly caught on to basketball, and it was a sport which intrigued him. James had already been touring post war Europe and had strong bonds with France. The club had lost gracefully to the French national team. Other clubs were beginning to take up the sport and hold friendly games with the Maryhill team but as yet it was not recognised as a sport, at least not in Scotland. Jimmy was determined to change that. He threw himself into the development and delivery of basketball as a sport with the same enthusiasm as ever. This effort soon paid off for the Maryhill Club as the sport slowly began to grow.

The Glasgow Union of Boys Clubs and the Central Council of Physical Recreation slowly became involved and by November 1946 the Western District of the Scottish Amateur Basketball Association was born.

There was also the ever growing calendar of events for the club itself. 6th March, the Glasgow Evening Times showed delight at the Maryhill Follies performance at the Lyric Theatre, Glasgow, on behalf of the Glasgow Association of Girls Clubs, especially their new act, The Mary- HillBillies.

Extract Evening Times

The British Legion Newmills sent a letter of thanks for the Maryhill Youth Club's displays and were astonished that monies raised were over £200, but were sad they were not in a position to give the club a donation. Instead they offered the club a position as Patrons and also one for James personally in return for his guidance, instructions and services, which were proudly accepted.

The 22nd March and another letter of appreciation, this time from the Association of Girls Clubs. *'Thank you once again at our inter-club display. Quite frankly I don't know what we would have done without you.'* Also *'regarding the world friendship, it has been decided at our executive meeting that your club will benefit by the £1.00 from our association so that at least will help with your bus fares.'*

Extract Evening Times

James had developed good relationships with those in the same field of work. They were becoming more accustomed to his ways, but they still moved away from him if his ideas were thought to be too radical.

The Maryhill Youth Club never turned down a cry of help to raise money for good causes no matter how small the cause.

28th March. The Bellshill Speaker. This newspaper organised a charity concert in aid of the Soldiers, Sailors and Airmen's Help Society. Sadly some of the acts were unable to attend at the last moment, but after a short phone call to the Maryhill Club the Maryhill Follies were booked, saving the day. Even though James and the club members worked hard, not all letters were of support. Some were criticising and damning especially over entertainment on a Sunday, as raising monies for worthy reasons should only occur through godly worship.

The reporter from the Evening Citizen had these words for James Muirhead.

'The story of Jimmy Muirhead's struggle at Maryhill to form a youth club is an amazing one - one that ranks with anyone anywhere. It took years to wean the tough youths of Maryhill. They laid in wait for him in the street, they threatened him with dire penalties if he didn't keep out and they even sent him memorial cards but Jimmy kept on. Now to mention Jimmy Muirhead's name in any other way than with respect in Maryhill would mean instant trouble for that person.' The report went on to say, *'It is one of the biggest youth clubs in the country. People come from all over to visit the club rooms and ask for advice. To crown all, he has brought out the talent that lies in each one of them and has created a concert party that is hard to beat.'* But the reporter was bothered by the outcry from people about the concert on the 30th March, even though it was to help those who had fought for country and freedom. Many were appalled that it was on the day of the Sabbath. This is what James wrote, *'I am amazed at the attitude of people, I wonder what some people think I am; I am running this concert and*

doing nothing wrong. I cannot find anything in the scriptures against Sunday concerts. If it's wrong on a Sunday then it's wrong on a Monday or any other night.'

The concert was a success, a full house. Tickets were priced at 2/6 (12½p) and 1/6 (7½p). The evening was filled with songs of Irish and other ballads, impressionists, musicians and dancers.

Sunday concerts continued and people complained but the Maryhill Club continued to perform. Letters of anger arrived at the club house and to the newspapers, expressing readers' distaste for the Maryhill Club's participation in Sunday entertainment.

On the 4th April a small article appeared in the Larnarkshire Gazette entitled, **'I'LL TRAVEL WITH JIMMY.'**

'It all boils down to this, when I think of some people I know who are so sure of heaven and consider a man like Mr Muirhead who has sacrificed his time and money all these years to help others, I would far rather travel down the road that is broad, than be taken to glory in a fiery chariot with an elder in the kirk.'

Even though the Sunday nights continued the dissension grew, but the concerts went on and the demand for the club increased.

The British Legion advertised their event. *'A MASSIVE PIPE BAND DISPLAY AND CONCERT will be presented by the Maryhill Youth Club Sunday the 23rd June. The Rev Jas. Martin will preside.'*

The club was busy preparing for a visit of international youth leaders. This was exciting new ground for the club. They had good and bad press over the Sunday concerts but the war was still in people's hearts and James had to take part with the Scottish Standing Conference of Voluntary Youth Organisations, to have a group of German youth leaders visit the Maryhill Club and receive guidance and tuition in youth

85

development !!!. Whatever controversy occurred over the event was eventually set aside.

July had come and the club was preparing for the two week camp. Jimmy was making changes to the club's structure. Some of the old members who had returned from the war were now outside the age limits of the club, so he began setting aside a part of the building to give them a lounge so they could have talks. He was delighted when fifty people turned up.

August 15th and the Evening News reports, *'The Maryhill Concert Party have an unbroken record of giving shows in aid of any good causes once a week since 1936* also *'Maryhill Club to appear at the opening night of the Youth rally in September, where there will be a display of basketball.'*

Letters of thanks just kept coming, one being from the Association of Girls Clubs for the display at the youth rally in September. October and the Glasgow Union of Boys Clubs gave thanks for the Maryhill Pipe Band's wonderful selection of music.

The club was putting the final touches to the performances for their annual display at the end of November in St Andrew's Halls but first they had a display of dancing on the 14th November at St James' Halls, Glasgow.

Christmas was soon approaching with another pantomime and the traditional Maryhill Christmas dinner of steak pie and chips and for dessert, basketball, the sport.

1948
BASKETBALL, THE SPORT AND
THE MARYHILL CLUB.

Basketball had grown over the last few years in Britain and the Maryhill Club was leading the way in Scotland. James ensured his team had proper coaching in the sport and they had their own personal trainer and masseur. As a result the Maryhill team developed their performance and ability as players and had serious recognition.

3rd January. The Bulletin had this to report. *'Neil Gillies of Maryhill Youth Club was playing for Scotland in the final Basketball Olympic trials in Birmingham'*. Sadly Neil did not make the British selection.

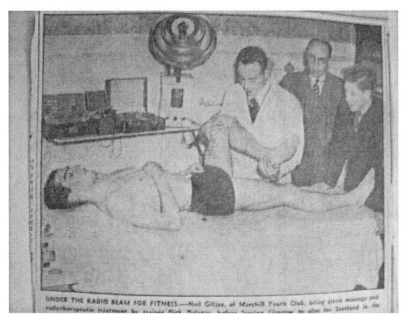

UNDER THE RADIO BEAM FOR FITNESS—Neil Gillies, of Maryhill Youth Club, being given massage and radiotherapeutic treatment

Extract The Bulletin

3rd January and a letter of thanks, this time from the Corporation of Glasgow Education Department for the splendid show for the children at a recent Christmas treat.

12th January. The Giffnock North Amateur Football Club also conveyed their thanks for the delightful performance of the Maryhill Youth Club's pipe band at their annual dance in the Tudor Ballroom.

James was devoting more time to basketball than ever, not just within the club but with the Union of Boys Clubs and the Central Council of Physical Recreation and other organisations, to promote and recognize basketball as a sport in Scotland.

21st January and basketball hit the headlines in the Evening Citizen. **'FIRST BASKETBALL LEAGUE OPENING.'** *'Glasgow will be the starting point in the development of basketball in Scotland as an organised sport. The first league has now been formed, the opening fixtures in a restricted first season schedule are due in 10 days.'*

Extract Evening Citizen

James was ecstatic with the concept. Teams such as Glasgow University and Jordanhill College, even the army, had

88

a team in the league and to top it all James was the interim secretary of the Western District of Scotland Basketball Association. The biggest problem the association faced was in expansion of the sport to younger teams. They needed to train officials in the game and they required more referees. James intervened immediately with an action plan.

21st January and the Evening Gazette reported this, *'Coaching classes for junior league officials start a week on Sunday at Maryhill Youth Club 43 Doncaster Street.'* The Maryhill basketball teams were training hard. In a few weeks time they were off to London to compete, and this time they were to be accompanied by their ladies' team who had been invited for a friendly match. Then it was back home to prepare for their match with the French national champions.

The pipe band had several events to attend and so had the Follies along with all their other preparations, scripts to write and learn and new acts to develop. Making costumes and scenery were all part of the process.

James and Helen still had the other activities that they ran nightly, cycling, wrestling, gymnastics, keep fit and many more. The club was now a full time occupation so it made sense that each section of the club should be run by club leaders to help share the workload under the watchful eye and guidance of James. These leaders were club members who had worked hard. James also felt it important that if the youths helped run and develop the club then everyone would benefit.

5th March Outram Press Social Club was having a meeting. Their topic of discussion was the Maryhill Basketball team and the forthcoming league match against the Outram Press. This is what was recorded in their minutes under the title, **'Introducing the Maryhill Y.C.'**

'The members of the basketball team are versatile athletes, playing football in the Scottish amateur league and being skilled gymnasts in great demand for displays. Trainer Dick Delany gives them ultra violet and infra-red treatment and massage regularly. Victor Mature has little on smiling Neil

Gillies, Captain and right guard of Maryhill Y.C. team. Redhead Ralph Cunningham too is an athlete of imposing stature. The most artistic player is probably Charlie Gray, left attacker. John Ross, the right attacker, scores freely, usually after a high jump to the basket. The centre, George Ramster, is very solidly built and is taller than he looks. George has not the experience of the others but nevertheless he takes his scores cleanly and coolly.

Our seniors meet Maryhill Y.C. on Friday the 12th March in the barrack gym. We have met Maryhill in many friendly and exhibition games with the score invariably ending with Maryhill winning by a very narrow margin. Spectators can expect speed, unselfish play, high scoring and excitement.'
While the Basketball world was debating and speculating, the other club members were working just as hard.

6th of April and the Maryhill Youth Club's pipe band had just returned home from London after a weekend event for the National Association of Boys Clubs. The pipe band had made such an impression that letters of thanks and appreciation from various people came flooding in.

Everyone was being caught up in basketball and the Lanarkshire Gazette was no different. They had organised an exhibition match between the Lanark Cameroonians and the Maryhill Club. On the 9th April, James sent letters out to Lanarkshire County Council and other youth groups. The game was one of excellence as Maryhill beat the army 47 to 34. It was the first time they had defeated them, but James was rather surprised by the game. He hadn't expected a large crowd but the fact there wasn't one youth leader present, not one grain of interest, had made him quite speechless.

There was no time to dwell on the event, as James received a letter confirming that the French national champions would be arriving on the 16th May to play the Maryhill's senior team. Helen immediately arranged for the team to have French lessons. The pipe band was off again back to London.

13th April and the club hits the headlines, again this time in the Evening News.

'MARYHILL TEAM TO TOUR NORMANDY'

'Maryhill returns the compliment in July to the French national team when they tour Normandy with two basketball teams and their senior soccer team. This is somewhat of an innovation even for this much travelled club.' But the paper had more to say, only this time the focus was on the pipe band. *'The pipe band had recently visited London for sports championships of the pre-service organisation where they played to 60,000 at Wembley and 10,000 at the Empire Pool. The skirl o' the pipes was one of the biggest successes of the meeting and the organisers immediately invited them to play next year'.*

James and Helen beamed with pride as they cut the articles from the papers and placed them in their ever growing scrap book. They were so proud of the achievements of the club, but especially of all the work and effort that each club member had given, for the credit belonged to the club members.

May was soon approaching and there was a lot to be done. The waiting list for the club was growing. During the war with the Army Cadet Force and the Girls Training Corps the club membership had grown to a thousand and now it was down to three hundred with a large waiting list. The club was open seven days a week all year round. Even at Glasgow Fair Fortnight the club was at camp. This club was exceptional in every way. They had seven football teams and their senior team of this year won the West of Scotland amateur cup.

Every March the Club put on a musical performance in the Lyric Theatre. Then there was a physical display at St Andrew's Halls held late October and then it was time for the Christmas pantomime with up to a hundred cast. There was the pipe band which consisted of fourteen pipers and eight drummers. They would like to have had a girls' pipe band but they didn't have any instruments yet. Then there was their junior pipe band with the youngest member being just nine and a half.

The 16th May had arrived, St Andrew's Halls was the venue. The French were agile and experienced players. The Maryhill team played a good game but not good enough as the

91

French beat them 54 to 12. The Maryhill Club over the next few days took the French team on a short tour of the lochs and of course a trip Doon the Watter to good auld Rothesay.

July had come and James was marching up and down outside the club house. Club members were arriving, and still there was no coach. This trip had originally started as a few days to Normandy but now they were scheduled for eight different towns over fourteen days. James sighed with relief as the bus came into sight and very soon all forty kilted club members were trundling out of Glasgow.

1st August and it was home at last. It had been a marathon event with champagne receptions in every town, and as they marched through the French streets led by their own pipers, bouquets were given to the girls. It was an amazing two weeks.

2nd August and the Bulletin printed this headline,

Swooping 'Plane Started Scots-French Match

THE "kick-off" was by aeroplane when Maryhill Youth Club played Alencon during a 14-day tour of Normandy. When the teams lined up, a 'plane swooped down and dropped the ball on the centre line.

This was one of many thrills recalled when the 40 kilted members of the club returned to Glasgow yesterday.

At eight towns, including Caen, Bayeux, and Deauville, the mayor and councillors headed a welcome from the people.

Champagne toasts were drunk at every ceremony, and as the visitors marched through the streets led by their pipers, bouquets were presented to the girls.

attracted enthusiastic audiences. In the Casino at Trouville every floor seat was occupied and 2000 crowded the balconies to see their show.

Another thrill was a visit to the horse stud near Alencon, where the sires of My Love and Royal Drake were admired.

Football and basketball matches were other features of the tour, and after the Olympic Games the club will be visited by M. Busnell, coach and trainer of the French Olympic basketball team.

Another visit to France has already been arranged—at Easter, when the club will go to Paris to play the leading basketball team

Extract The Bulletin

92

'SWOOPING PLANE STARTED SCOTS-FRENCH MATCH'

'The 'kick off' was by aeroplane when Maryhill Youth Club played Alencon during a fourteen day tour of Normandy. When the teams lined up a plane swooped down and dropped the ball on the centre line. After the Olympic Games the club will be visited by M. Bisnell the coach and trainer of the French Olympic team.'

This event was to change life for the Maryhill Club, as they would spend many years touring post war Europe.

The Maryhill Club began its final preparations for their annual display. The pipe band was rehearsing for another commitment, this time in Edinburgh where they were to play for H.R.H The Duke of Gloucester for his official visit to Edinburgh on the 13th November. James and Helen however were off to North Berwick to address a weekend conference in youth work for the Central Council of Physical Recreation, for which they received £2:10/ (£2.50) expenses, with permission to give what monies had not been spent to the club as a donation.

Pipe Band

93

1949
MARYHILL INVADES EUROPE

Fifteen years had passed since that first night in Garscube Road. There had been lots of controversy along the way, first with the church then the open doors policies. Then raised eyebrows and outcry of debauchery when he allowed the boys and girls to train and perform together.

Only James would take the Maryhill Club on tour of post war Europe, and make it successful. Most of the young people of that era had never been out of Glasgow never mind abroad. These youngsters were going to have experiences that only the rich could have given their children, Europe in spring and summer, new cultures and experiences that we take for granted in this day and age. This year was to be the beginnings of a silent invasion from the Maryhill Club in football, basketball, pipe band and the concert party. They would take Europe by storm as sportsmen and women and performers. Touring Denmark, Italy, Spain, Holland and France, the club would reach heights of international acclaimed recognition and would be invited to advise and develop clubs abroad.

The club was preparing for the yearly commitments when an unusual request came in from Glenmore Lodge in Aviemore. During the Second World War the Cairngorm Mountains were the most suitable terrain for commando units to train in cross-country skiing. Numerous units were trained in mountain warfare. After the war it became a place for the rich.

Now The Central Council of Physical Recreation and the Cooperate of Glasgow Education were part of a trial being run in the Cairngorms. They had taken part in climbing and mountaineering training for young students which was a great success, but they wanted to open this up for the secondary school children so they asked James and his club to take part.

Pioneering was a popular activity in the club and James took all of this in his stride as he unveiled his latest new project, fencing, and The Times picked up the story.

'YOUNG SWORDSMEN'

'Maryhill is again pioneering and this time to introduce fencing into the youth movement. A demonstration will be held on Tuesday night at the Maryhill Club house by the Scottish Amateur Fencing Union'.

23rd February and the Daily Record also printed a similar piece, with pictures of Maryhill Club member, Betty Walkinshaw, making a hit on Edinburgh fencing team's Doris Brotherton.

Extract Daily Record

The basketball team was on the move again and were given a warm welcome from North Shields Centre before their big match against the local team also on the same day.

4th Feb. and Citizen News printed this article. **'26 GUINEA PIGS FROM MARYHILL'**- *'Glenmore Lodge Inverness-shire, the experimental centre for open-air activities established by the Central Council of Physical Recreation has up to now been almost exclusively for the people who can take a* *week off work- the length of the complete course. If this weekend comes off, then all that will change.'*

9th February and the Bulletin gave the Maryhill Club a centre feature with photographs of the Cairngorms and Glenmore Lodge along with club members, Mary Walsh and Irene Linn and Bernard and Dick Gowers of the Craig Dubh Mountain Club.

10th March and the Daily Record printed these headlines, **'40 City School Girls Enjoy a Millionaire's holiday.'**

'Quite a while ago Maryhill established precedence. There's nothing unusual in that – Maryhill Club is always establishing precedents. This particular one however was especially interesting, it became the first club to try out the climbing and skiing facilities at what had been considered as the rich man's domain- Glenmore Lodge. This experiment was so successful and Maryhill had lots of fun that other parties are taking the trial to Aviemore.'

Extract The Daily Record

March and the basketball league was in full swing. The competition was high for the leadership of the western district championships but Maryhill was just in the lead. Two years ago when the Scottish Basketball Association started, there was just a handful of teams. Now there were ninety teams taking part in leagues and knock out competitions through the four main areas of the country, but soon the season would end with a national championship in May

The Maryhill Club was a fulltime occupation for all.

1st March and the Daily Mirror commented on this, in this article - *'Mr Muirhead, who took charge of the Maryhill Club as a hobby, now finds the work of running his decorating business is now his hobby.'*

The Central Council of Physical Recreation had the Maryhill members involved in the experiment in the Cairngorms. They also called on the club's physical display team, for an event called the Kaleidoscope of the keep-fit movement, in St Andrew's Halls on the 30th of March and then again on the 7th of April for the Girls Union of Clubs.

21st April and basketball hits the headlines in the Daily Mirror, this time with a picture of Maryhill Club's own Mary Walsh playing basketball. *'Mary Walsh, 16, of Glasgow is an all round sports girl. After her day's work in a book publishing office she fences or goes ice-skating and she loves rock climbing. In July, Mary will be going to Paris with the Maryhill Youth Club team to play basketball'.*

Extract Daily Mirror

'TOP OF THEIR LEAGUE BUT STILL LEARNING' was the heading of the Evening Citizen.

'Maryhill Youth Club have won the Western District Senior League. They are the favourites for the Scottish title. Yet tomorrow they go on Easter tour to learn more about the game. They will play Barry, near Cardiff then at Warrington against the U.S.A Air Force before going on to play at Oldham and Rochdale's Grey.'

The basketball team were back from their Easter tour of England and Wales and there was much to talk about. The Evening Citizen on the 23rd April couldn't help but report it under the title **'BASKETBABEL'** - *'In their tour of England and Wales, in one town they encountered, had a home team of Lithuanians, who spoke no English. In another town their opponents included two Americans and an American referee who changed his strip at half time and joined the players. Despite this Maryhill won 52-12. Jim Muirhead takes a dim view of the globalism as he does of the East of Scotland Select that the Maryhill team meet tonight at Falkirk. The team comprises of mainly Americans and Poles.'*

Glasgow had long since lacked an indoor sport centre which was always available and James' club was the driving force behind a scheme to provide such a centre. In the Pleasuredome, New City Road, they were making good use of it. 25th April and the Pleasuredome was the venue for the Maryhill basketball team and the American team Destroyer Gzatts.

May was here and the Scottish Basketball season reached its peak and the Evening Citizen reported the event. **'GALLANT MARYHILL'** - *'Kelvin Hall was where the junior and senior basketball cup finals were held. Although Maryhill seniors lost the cup to Edinburgh University 26-37 they established themselves as the outstanding all Scottish team of the year. Like most teams who have beaten them this year Edinburgh University was largely composed of Americans.'*

June was approaching. The club members were training hard, rehearsing a new act for the up and coming event at Patrick Thistle sports ground on the 18th of June. The Maryhill Youth Club would put on a spectacular display of club swinging and a circus parade in conjunction with the Central Council of Physical Recreation. Then soon they were off to France for two weeks. This time they were going to trade experiences with the French basketball team. The French would coach the Maryhill team, and the Maryhill soccer team would coach the French team.

The Junior Pipe Band would also be busy as the British Sailors' Society had asked for their help at Flag Day. 28th of July Glasgow Flag Day came. The pipe band played and other members of the Maryhill Club sold flags all over Glasgow. The British Sailors' Society was delighted with the help. The amount of money raised on the day was £487.

The Maryhill Club had returned from France and as always James had brought the French newspaper articles home for the scrap book. The press were delighted on their return

The Times, Evening News and The Citizen ran this article, **'THREE 1914-18 WAR BUGLES PLAYED THEIR WELCOME.'**

'One inch high headlines are a rarity these days of merge newsprint, and when one of the Glasgow youth clubs get them, it's really something. They visited several towns in France. One place was Plougonvelin. They gave the club an official welcome and played them in on three rather battered bugles from the 1914 war. Other towns had played welcomes with big brass bands. The Maryhill Youth Club say that these three bugles touched them the most.'

James and the Maryhill Club had a wonderful time but they soon noticed that things were very different regarding the workings of French authorities, especially when to start or even finish an event. At Cherbourg their Scottish concert was due to begin at 9.15 p.m. As they were just starting an official dinner at quarter to eight, the concert didn't start till after 10p.m. The audience weren't perturbed; they just sat patiently waiting, which was a wonder as most concerts and games brought crowds of up to 5,000. At this concert the Maryhill girls did a dancing exhibition at 1.30a.m and the club still had a game of basketball to follow. But it was the little village of Plougonvelin that would stay with the hearts of the club members for a long time. They had been the first official Scottish party ever to visit. They were also the first Britons to visit the village cemetery and lay wreaths on the graves of three unknown Flyers. But there was more news.

There was more travelling to be done as the club set off again to Millport, this time on the Isle of Cumbrae to take part in a gala week of gymnastics, vaulting, club swing, keep fit, pipe band and much more. During this time there were other preparations going on. There was a new pantomime to put together and the annual display, a second trip to Glenmore Lodge that September before the Gala concert in November by the Maryhill Follies for the Union of Girls Clubs. The club had earned this year's Christmas dinner of steak pie and chips.

Maryhill Club in France

1950
LARGER THAN LIFE

At the end of 1949, James resigned from the Western District of Scotland Basketball Association and took up the position as secretary of The Scottish Amateur Basketball Association. In October of the previous year he had also made some changes to the club's structure and had opened a section for the young mums, which had been so well attended that he was in the process of planning a grandparent section. Since they were no longer strictly a youth club it was time the Maryhill Youth Club incorporated their new name The Maryhill Club into its logo, which was reflected in their monthly magazine. This also happens to be the front cover of this book.

The original magazine was one page of A4 folded in half and completely filled with news. There was just a donation to receive it. Now the magazine consisted of a minimum ten pages and there was a subscription of 4/- (20p) with free posting.

January was a time of planning and preparation for the main events within the club. There was already a booking for the concert party for the end of January organized by the ward committee, who were raising funds for the elderly.

14th January and The Weekly News printed this headline, **'Fiery-cross kilties going to Spain.'** *'At the Glasgow fair, a party of 40 kilted Scots youths will leave Glasgow for Spain. They'll sail as passengers aboard a cargo boat. Many will carry bagpipes.*
Making their headquarters in Madrid, the Scots will play basketball and football games against crack Spanish amateur teams.'

Basketball was still a major part of the club's life and for Scotland. James was behind the biggest battle for recognition of the sport and he was waging war with his troops, the basketball players. The expansion of popularity of the sport was being hindered by the lack of sizeable accommodation, but James had managed to secure again Friday nights at the Pleasure Dome in

Glasgow, which was one of Scotland's largest indoor stadiums. For the Maryhill team's home games and for the first time in Scottish history of this sport, there would be a small charge for spectators of 6d. (2½p). The Pleasure Dome was to see more of the Maryhill Club when they also started lessons that month in what James called the basketball nursery. To qualify all you had to do was be a beginner and not a member of a club.

Extract Evening Times

21st January and this time the People's Journal was hot on the trail with this headline, '**Full of Bright Ideas.**'

'A club for the Grannies and Grandpas is to be run by the Maryhill Youth Club. This club will have afternoon meetings for indoor games-draughts, dominoes and chess with film shows and talks with demonstrations. The club's premises for indoor activities are 43 Doncaster Street and their sports ground is Caldercuilt Park. Their basketball section is to have its own outdoor court which will be fitted with floodlighting equipment

for night practise. Maryhill Youth Club teams have demonstrated the sport in Wales, France, Holland and all over England, and at Easter the team will tour Ireland before going to Spain in July. Cyclists, the Maryhill Wheelers are training on the latest continental lines using rollers made in the club's workshop.'

February was a quiet month. There was the opening for the first group of Maryhill grandparents who enjoyed their afternoon activities. The club was different from most in the Glasgow district, as the club would meet as often as members required and activities would be according to their needs. The grandparents would be involved in decisions regarding activities. There would be a social activity on a monthly basis. There were forty five members over the age of sixty five and James was able, should it be required, to accommodate up to a hundred and fifty members.

Grandpa's Section

James was also at this time an active member of nineteen national bodies including executives of the British Olympics and the Central Council for Physical Recreation.

The concert party was rehearsing for the old folk's concert as well as a musical recital in the Lyrics Hall in March. The Indian Club team was going through its paces for a performance for the Scottish Association of Girls' Clubs and the fencing team was preparing for an inter-club display also at the Lyric Theatre in late April.

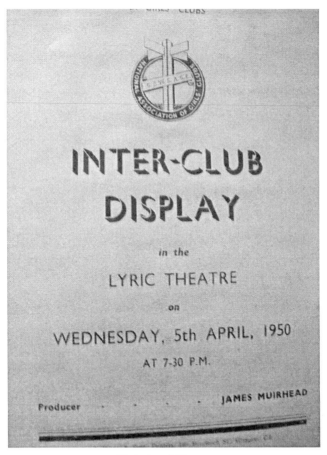

Original Poster

The pipe band had given a performance in the Florida Glasgow Cinema. Grafton Hutchinson of the Children's Cinema Club department had sent the usual thank you letter, except that one small paragraph caught James' attention, *'I was given to understand that you took considerable personal trouble on Saturday morning itself to pick up all the boys, I do appreciate this very much, I was also told that in the flurry the empty taxi went off with the big drum still strapped on behind. I had wondered during the performance why we had no bass drum, I hope you got it back alright.'* It was refreshing to know that even James had his moments of oops!

28th April and Lanarkshire Gazette had this simple headline, '**Maryhill Youth Club.**'

'The Maryhill Youth Club with kind permission of its leader Mr James Muirhead will visit the community centre on Thursday and put on one of their shows to help the Imperial Chemical Industries Limited (I.C.I.) get its pipe band. This is a fine gesture on Jimmy's part'.

2nd May the Glasgow Evening Times had this headline, '**Well Booked.**'

'The Maryhill Club are helping all sorts of good causes, not only in Glasgow but everywhere else by giving shows and displays. Among the recent shows were those for old age pensioners in Hamilton Hill and another later for their summer outing. The club continues to open every afternoon and week nights.'

The basketball team was booked for a demonstration in the Corn Exchange. The opposition were drawn from Americans working in this country, called the Latter Day Saints. The game would be controlled by Mr Charles Wall, an international referee. David Pentlands of Maryhill Club was team captain, and in 1948 was the captain of the Scottish Olympic team.

12th May and their concert for I.C.I was here. Can you vision a company of youths and girls having a spot of harmony together? Well two girls, Jeannette Dunn and Anne Kerr, can be singled out especially for their dancing and singing. Mary

Mclean, as a comedienne, was an outstanding feature of the show. These girls were not only talented performers, but all round athletes.

19th May and The Evening Citizen printed an article on the activities of groups and clubs in general. These were the reporter's comments.

'It is doubtful if a youth club is doing itself any good by taking on so many interests that it finds itself unable to cope with them. It is one thing having a large and varied programme of successful activities - another having the same large programme of activities, each of which are supported by a mere handful of members. But in the case of the Maryhill Club it seems it could take on the task of paying off the national debt and still make headway. The problem with this club is a housing shortage, so what does the club do –discontinue some classes? No - what they are going to do is launch a development campaign to raise £3,000, for example a sale of work, two major shows and displays and a minor charity day (similar to what the students do). Date for raiding the public pockets will be 24th August.'

12th June and the Evening News ran a full page article on James and the club. This is an extract with the headline, **'Maryhill's Happy Autocrat.'**

'Muirhead is a sharp balding little man of 40. He is on so many executives that he is beginning to lose count but Maryhill is his dream child. About three times in 10 years he has decided to have a night off and went into his garden, but by 9 o'clock in the evening a funny feeling came over him and he started to turn green. Mrs Muirhead said, 'Maybe we should go down to the club.' In the back streets of Maryhill, Muirhead is loved. He has one son but his family runs close on 600....grannies and toddlers and the rest, he is a happy autocrat.'

28th June and Grangemouth was the place to be, Zetland Park to be precise, where there was pipe band, dancing, keep fit, fencing, Indian Club swinging team, who were one of the best in

Scotland and basketball by the famous Maryhill Youth Club. By now the basketball team was boasting five Scottish international players.

James and Helen in Spain

The team came home excited and tired from the Spanish continental tour, in which they had managed to squeeze a special request visit to Normandy before returning home to Glasgow. James was to learn on his return that the Pleasure Dome where his basketball team trained had been sold, and was no longer available to anyone. This was a blow as the champions' teams, both male and female, of the Yugoslavia basketball team were coming in October to play. He turned to the help of the papers. On the 3rd August the Glasgow Evening News printed the story. This is a small extract. *'Little wonder that Mr Muirhead has that desperate gleam in his eye. In the few years basketball teams have been in existence they have reached world class. You don't make the grade in any sport without terrific effort. Had this happened to a continental team training, quarters would immediately have been available and a tidy subsidy given. All Mr Muirhead asks is the let of a building, as he puts it, four walls and a roof anywhere. So if you happen to know of a vacant four walls please call.'*

The paper the following week ran another article titled **'Basketball Search.'** With only seven weeks to the Yugoslavians' arrival, they had still not secured premises. The reporter wrote, *'He is not optimistic for the quarters he desires as they must be 100ft long and 60ft wide by at least 20ft high, He thinks there might be an old garage, factory or foundry or some such place in Glasgow of the dimensions desired which can be rented or purchased. The Yugoslavian tour is on for seven weeks where they will play at Aberdeen, Edinburgh and London. If Glasgow is not included it would be bad advertisement for the city and the respect for the basketball players.'*

September 22nd and the Maryhill Basketball team had arrived in Ireland for a game against the Americans working there, they were none other than the Latter Day Saints. The Latter Day Saints were outstanding in their game play. I quote from an Irish paper. *'They have been undefeated this year and their team captain Dick Sagara is six feet of muscle and speed.'*

They said this about Maryhill. *'One of Scotland's leading teams has come over to especially meet the Latter Day Saints in an attempt to lower their colour.'* The result was Maryhill 48 – Latter Day Saints 39. (Way hay for the Maryhill Club ☺)

Original poster

Another fine match was against the American Air Force champions called the Bullets; they had these kind words for the Maryhill team, *'Even though they lost by only two points, they should be called the Maryhill Cannons.'*

James had resolved the situation of the Yugoslavian team. He hired the Kelvin Hall for the club's annual display and just included the match. He was to be thwarted in his attempts as the Yugoslavians decided that unless Maryhill team meet their full travel expenses they wouldn't come. The Sporting Record printed this. '**Yugoslav tour off.**' *'The Yugoslavian authorities phoned James Muirhead and offered to make the journey to Scotland if he paid them the sum of £380 on arrival at London. This last minute offer was refused by Mr Muirhead and the basket ball match will be played at the Kelvin Hall instead with American Air Force team."*

The Club's annual display went without a hitch. They managed a circus performance, and with little rest, their final preparations for the annual pantomime were then under way.

The Christmas parties this year would have to be divided into three sections, junior, seniors and one for the old folks.

The Indian club team, however, were under a strict training regime under the coaching guidance of Helen Muirhead as the team prepared for the Scottish Championships free standing event.

The new club choir was now adding their talents to the club services and had been appointed for three concerts. The concert party was preparing for a concert on 11th January next year, for the Woodside Old folks treat at Woodside Hospital.

The basketball teams of Junior A and B, as well as the senior team were in practise for the League cups. The football teams A and B were holding their own but had not been successful at winning the amateur league. All in all it had been a busy and eventful time.

Indian Club Team

New Maryhill Choir

1951-1953
A QUIET TIME

The next three years were a time of, should one say, relaxation for the club. James was spending his time maturing the club's activities as well as developing his other pursuits.

The club had grown so fast it was time to stay still just for a little while. There wasn't much documentation, well nothing of much interest, but here are some of the highlights of the years.

1951 started the same as any other year with January shows and pantomime. The concert party and the pipe band were starting the year with a full diary of events as was the basketball team with demonstrations and league games.

Ayr was the first port of call for the basketball team although there were 150 teams in existence in Scotland, 50 of those were from Glasgow. The sport however was comparatively new in Ayr.

This game was claimed to be the second fastest on foot in the world, with ice hockey holding the top position. The Maryhill Club continued to promote basketball in Scotland. With the help of King's Park team they put on a spectacular demonstration hoping that the youth groups in Ayr would form a league of their own, especially since the American troops based at Prestwick had their own team. The demonstration proved to be very popular with a full turn out of spectators at Ayr Academy Assembly Hall. The score was Maryhill 39 King's Park 35.

25th February and The Evening Times printed this headline, '**SECRETARY BRINGS OFF THREE GOOD COUPS**'

'National secretary Mr J.Muirhead brought off three big coups this week to bring basketball more into the limelight north of the border. The first is American service men from units from Europe and the Middle East will combine a U.S.A.A.F. select to meet Scotland in the Waverly Market Edinburgh on March 29th.

A return visit will be made on May 15th where they will play a national side at Ayr ice rink. Third achievement is a series of talks on basketball soon to be given by the B.B.C. with plans to televise the Scotland vs Wales International and all other big games.'

The grandparents' section of the club was going strong and on the 5th June they were off to Largs for their annual outing.

July was now approaching with another tour to France and Spain with the basketball teams and the pipe band.

12 September and the Consulate de France, J. Taddei wrote to James regarding men and women of French nationality living in Glasgow, and the possibility of coming to the Maryhill Club for fencing and basketball, as the club had given much help to France with their young men and women.

October and James found himself on the committee of the Glasgow & West of Scotland Association of Girls' Clubs.

November of this year, James began the task of arranging a coaching scheme in Ayrshire and Dumfries-shire with the hope of basketball teams being formed within the next year.

Basketball Team

The club premises at Doncaster Street were deteriorating. It needed renovation and expansion to work to its full potential, and plans were being developed to increase fund raising for this purpose.

29th March, and the Evening Times printed this. **'GRANDPARENTS' MITE'**

'Founded for youth the Maryhill Club occupies a unique position, in that it caters for all ages from tiny tots to grandparents. The grandparents' and the mothers' sections have raised on average £7 per month. What have the youths to say to that?'

James needed to remind the public of what the Maryhill Club did and, as before, he approached the newspapers. The club got a visit from the Daily Mail and on 29th April it ran this headline. **'THEY ALL PLAY THE GAME IN THIS COMMUNITY'** by Ken Graham.

'I walked into the gymnasium, a group of young men and women dressed in white jackets and meshed masks were thrusting and parrying foil and sabre. They stopped for a minute and removed the masks; I always imagined fencing as the sport of a retired army officer. Now I know differently, there were clerks and cashiers, apprentices and office boys taking up the en grande position with the grace and skill of Cyrano de Bergerac's. I then wandered into the lounge where I found Peter watching a game of dominoes between some of his cronies.

Tea? Yes, I had a cup of tea. It cost 1d (½p) and came from the canteen which is staffed by members of the mother's group. Upstairs a group of girls were finishing a tap dancing class, the night before the room had been used by the forty member pipe band.

Just round the corner I found another room in which 46 year old, Fred Quick, a printer and qualified masseur was helping ease one of the grandpa's rheumatism. He also keeps the basketball, football and other sporting teams of the club in shape. It was a fine evening when I called and most of the young people were out cycling, playing basketball or training. Basketball is one of the club's features, they have collected trophies all over the continent, but team coaches are worried this year as both A and B teams have reached the semi finals. If both go through there could be some keen rivalry within the club members.

Other club activities include mountaineering, skiing, sailing and hiking. On my way out I ran into Peter. He said, 'It's a grand place. I'm never out of it. The wife says I should bring my bed here. In my days we only had Sunday School and the Magic Lantern. The concert party too is kept busy to aid charities. Sometimes as many as two shows a week and the pipe band is always being invited to play at garden fetes and charity shows.'

The public response was poor to this article. A few donations came in through the paper and from people who had been moved by the article. Basketball was still a large feature of the club. In November The Evening Times had this headline, **'PUBLIC ARE TAKING TO BASKETBALL.'**

'Since Mr Muirhead, of Maryhill Youth Club introduced the game on a competitive basis, clubs have been started in Edinburgh, Dundee, Perth, Aberdeen in fact in almost every town and city in Scotland.

It was largely due to Mr Muirhead's efforts that Britain was represented at the European Championships in Paris last year. He has pioneered the development of basketball in recent years and the excellent standard of play in his own club has put it on equal footing with the best in Britain.'

Grandparents' Section

The Maryhill Club was still maintaining a low key but on the 27th March the Evening Times held this headline, **'BARGE HOLIDAY FOR THIS MARYHILL CLUB.'** *'You can always bank on James Muirhead to think up a surprise for his club, the Maryhill Club. But this time it is something that will appeal to everyone for its spirit of adventure, a journey by barge through Holland, West Germany and Belgium'.*

Extractl Evening News

'On July the 18th Mr Muirhead and his wife Helen and forty boys and girls of the club, will start out on what will be the strangest holiday of their lives. For two weeks the barge will be their home. With a Dutch crew to sail it and cook to provide the meals what more could you ask? During the journey they will stop at various ports and play basketball games with local youth clubs.

This holiday was magnificent even by today's standards. However the matter of the premises was becoming pressing. James had no option but to hire an electrician, and also there was the roof to address, and the list grew and so the fundraising started in earnest. The Club relied on the annual show as the main fundraiser to maintain the club from year to year, with various donations acquired through the year. Now the preparation for an additional Christmas show was under way.

There was one other problem that had surfaced over the last few months and that was one of youth delinquency. The police were concerned with the increasing numbers of youths who were committing acts of vandalism and other crimes. It was far more serious in the suburban areas in Glasgow. James was well aware of the rising problem even in Maryhill. It was time to extend his club into other areas and have premises that could cope with extra numbers, and after due consideration he decided, instead of repairing Doncaster Street he would just strip the club back to the bare walls, and remodel the club, and that's exactly what he did.

OUT WITH THE OLD IN WITH THE NEW

8th January 'HE'S BUILDING A £10,000 CLUB – WITHOUT MONEY!' was the headline in the Evening News. Jim Currie wrote, *'The man who pooh-poohs the phrase "Juvenile delinquents" is tearing down the material structure of 20 years' youth work and starting a-fresh. He is James Muirhead founder president of the Maryhill Club. His objective is to make room for the problem age category of our times, the nines to thirteens.*

The whole interior of the club premises are being ripped out and renewed. A second storey will be added to the building to house classrooms and lounges. The ground floor will contain one huge gymnasium

"What will that cost?" I asked.

"Oh about £10,000," he replied.

"How much money do you have?"

"None."

"When will the work start?"

"It has started."

These brief answers give you the Muirhead touch-action. Mr Muirhead has firm ideas about these problem children. "It is all a question of environment and circumstances," he said. "You will see the youngsters any evening scrambling around parked motor cars when they should either be in bed or doing something useful. I think the youth club is the answer."'

There was already a 900 strong membership of the Maryhill Club, but with the new construction he could accommodate at least another 200 members. This would allow him to tackle the problematic youths who were running amok.

His target bunch was in the age group of the nines to thirteens. James believed in intervention. If this age group of children were to be nurtured he knew they would learn the spirit of comradeship and fair play before their lives became marred with court appearances. Youth clubs are supposed to give young people the outlet for their ambitions and emotions. Without this they could be led astray in the streets.

Work continued at the club, but it was slow as James refused to close the premises, so the builders had to work round the club members, which was no easy task.

Extract Evening News

4th June and a letter arrived from James Robertson M.B.E., J.P.

'*Dear Mr Muirhead,*

I was greatly impressed by what I saw on Monday evening and I feel I must become one of the hundred business men and professional men to whom you appealed. I therefore enclose my cheque for £15 and with it my best wishes for continued success.

Kind regards.

Yours sincerely

James Robertson.

/*Enc. cheque £15*

Cash   £10

£25

This was indeed a handsome donation as the average wage was £6.00 per week.

July was approaching fast, and preparation for the forthcoming trip was under way. This certainly wouldn't have the flare of the Dutch barge holiday of last year. Let me tell you, if the Scot is a popular figure in La Belle France you can give much of the credit to the Maryhill Club. That summer they were off on another of their goodwill holidays which have done so much towards making friends across the water. Can you picture a bus carrying a pipe band, a basketball team, a concert party and a keep fit team all the way from Glasgow to Normandy? That will be the Maryhill Club. It certainly wasn't the cheapest way to travel but it certainly was the easiest considering the luggage and equipment they would carry. The pipers had always been a big hit in France, but what seemed to be more popular was the tap dancing act in the club's concert party. Tap dancing is practically unknown in provincial areas of France.

Extract Evening News

Can you imagine seventeen days in a bus touring Normandy and Brittany with forty five club members whose average age was fifteen? Ahhh!!! Giving concerts and displays and of course playing basketball. The club was renowned for its excellence in entertainment and athletic attributes and had travelled the continent every year since 1946. No wonder they were so popular.

10th August and the Maryhill Club was in a frenzy as club members, parents and friends, descended in droves at Doncaster Street with a definite mission to complete the alteration to the club, in preparation of the club's biggest show ever, their twenty first anniversary performance. James was pulling out all the stops as club members painted and decorated, learned lines and dances, put hammer to nails, polished routines, as well as inventing and performing something spectacular, the likes of which had never been seen before.

The event was approaching fast. James, for the first time, had to make the show a ticket only event and they only had until Saturday to complete the necessary work.

Principle guests were the Lord Inverclyde, magistrates, councillors and a number of financial and influential business men.

13th August and The Evening Times printed this head line Maryhill, **'DO IT IN STYLE.'**

'Have you ever seen dancing in roller skates, no well you'll see it on Saturday at Doncaster Street if you have been lucky enough to get a ticket. But undoubtedly the biggest attraction will be the basketball match between Maryhill team and the pick of Normandy. IT'S A RECORD: - Now a 1000 strong, the Maryhill Club has left a mark for service which you would find difficulty in equalling anywhere. During the war it formed its own concert party and gave over a 1000 concerts. It had a boys' messenger service for the city, sick nursing unit and was the only youth club in Britain to have its own army cadet unit. Now that's impressive even for today. When Mr Muirhead started his boys' club twenty-one years ago he had great

visions, now look at the results. A community centre which caters for age groups from nothing to ninety six. This may sound fantastic, but the proof is in the fact that one of the club members is expecting and has already enrolled it.'

The members had been working furiously on the alterations getting ready for Saturday night's big show, but this was such an extensive face lift, as removing a balcony and putting in a new floor takes time and money. The work was only half way through and they still needed £5,000 more to complete the job.

17th August and the show was a success. The Sunday Mail printed the headlines, '**A MARYHILL CLUB COMES OF AGE.**'

'James Muirhead and his wife Helen began a local youth club with 20 members and the use of a small one-roomed shop. Last night the same man watched some of his 1000 club members cramming a Glasgow drill hall to celebrate coming of age. The Maryhill Club had plenty to celebrate and made no bones about it with teams of brightly clad athletes, pipe bands, roller-skaters and young gymnasts. A Maryhill and France basketball game and comedy turns followed each other in well drilled precision, amid the roars of laughter and applause from aunties, uncles, cousins and friends lining the hall.'

The event was a financial success and the club had raised an amazing £3,000 but they still needed another £2000 minimum. They would just have to put on an extended Christmas show to help raise the extra money.

The Evening Times was more than just a paper; it was a great supporter of youth work. Thankfully for the last few years the Evening Times had paid for the use of the Lyric Hall in Glasgow for the club's Christmas show, and would also pay for the extended show. In fact the Evening Times worked in conjunction with the club over different events such as 'Youth in Action.'

Relaxation was something of a rarity in the Muirhead household. James' outlet was his garden. Helen enjoyed the moment when she could sit in her armchair and knit. At times she felt envious of the grandmothers' and mothers' section as they spent the afternoons knitting and chatting, but from this knitting came a solution to the money situation.

The club had been working hard with fundraising but they needed far more and Helen's answer to increase funds was simple 'let's knit.' With the grandmothers' and mothers' sections full cooperation the club purchased two knitting machines. The Evening News was soon spreading the word with this headline on the 9th December, '**KNITTING THEIR WAY OUT OF DEBT**' by Jim Currie.

'Maryhill Club's annual revue which opened on Wednesday night can be successfully counted on to draw the crowds until next Tuesday. Behind the scenes however lies a different story. Mr Muirhead widely known as the founder-president of the Maryhill Club is a disappointed man. He told me, "It would appear to be easier to collect money for white mice and stray cats than it is to collect it for youth work. Well the Maryhill Club isn't in the habit of sitting around, they need £2,000 and they are determined to get it or bust and they are setting up a knitting factory to do it. So far they have two knitting machines producing the goods. You can knit a jumper in an hour and a pair of socks in just 20 minutes. There have been certain people out there who have helped us, but on the whole it is not like that. If we were raising money for white mice and stray cats we would be flooded with people wanting to give us donations. But that's just the way people are made."

Helen Muirhead

126

Christmas was here at last and the club's Christmas party was in full swing when Moira Loan, the club captain, paused the proceeding to make a special announcement. The whole hall was silent as Moira asked James and Helen to the floor before speaking.

"With love and thanks from all here at the Maryhill Youth Club we would like to present you both with this gift as a gesture of thanks for all your hard work but also to mark this special 21 year anniversary of the club." The couple were presented with a beautiful canteen of cutlery with bone handles in a wooden box lined with royal blue satin.

Happy Birthday Maryhill.

1955
THE BIRTH OF THE TEENAGER

This year started much the same as any other, with concerts for the old folk. The basketball team had won their semi finals and was preparing for the finals.

The alterations to the club were just about finalised and already, as James promised, it was taking in more members of the ages of nine to thirteen year olds.

Something was brewing. There was a new youth element on the streets and it was growing fast, a revolution of young people who no longer wanted to be miniature versions of their parents. They wanted excitement, to be able to express themselves in their own way, their own style, to break out of these boring roles that society dictated. It was the teenager in the form of the Teddy Boy.

The original British Teddy Boy was typified by young men who wore clothes inspired by the styles of the Edwardian period, which Saville Row tailors had tried to re-introduce after World War II. Originally known as Cosh Boys, the name Teddy Boy came about after a 1953 Daily Express newspaper headline shortened Edward to Teddy and coined the term Teddy Boy (also known as Ted). The Teddy Boy style started in London in the early 1950s and rapidly spread across the UK, and then became strongly associated with American rock 'n' roll music. It should be noted, however, that Teddy Boys were around before rock 'n' roll music became popular in Britain, and were a totally British phenomenon as opposed to the other styles worn in countries such as the United States. Although there had been youth groups with their own dress codes called Scuttlers in 19th century Manchester and Liverpool, Teddy Boys were the first youth group in England to differentiate themselves as teenagers, helping to create a youth market.

The Teddy Boy style and trend arose as income increased after the Second World War. Traditionally, Teddy Boy clothing has been typified with long drape jackets, usually in dark shades, generally with a black velvet collar and pocket flaps and high-waist drainpipe trousers, often exposing the socks. The predominant favoured footwear were highly polished Oxford shoes, chunky brogues, or crepe-soled shoes, often suede (known as brothel creepers). A high-necked loose collar on a white shirt (known as a Mr. B. collar because it was often worn by jazz musician Billy Eckstine) was complemented by a narrow Slim Jim tie, or Maverick tie, and a brocade silk patterned waistcoat. These clothes were mostly tailor-made at great expense and paid for through weekly instalments. Preferred hairstyles included long, strongly-moulded greased-up hair with a quiff at the front and the side combed back to form a duck's tail at the rear. Another style was the Boston, in which the hair was greased straight back and cut square across at the nape.

For teenagers of today it is probably impossible to imagine living in post war Britain. Rationing was still in force, and for the youth of the working population employment began at fifteen for a forty-eight hour week, to earn less than £4. Clothes, for example, were conservative and mainly muted. Cars were black or dark shades, the likes of sparkling metal flake paint had not yet arrived. Even the newspapers were devoid of colour and clearly life for many could be exceedingly down beat. The hugely successful Festival of Britain exhibition in 1951, promoted as a 'tonic for Britain', and the coronation of Elizabeth II in 1953, gave something of a lift to the country but did little for the youth of the land. Countless numbers were at a loose end without purpose; they had no role models, few aspirations or real identity.

Juvenile crime was escalating as it is often said the devil makes mischief for idle hands. He probably had a ball inciting the most notorious breed of wild youth that emerged from the period. This was the Edwardian Brigade, the drape coat fraternity. They were the new villains of the time, taking over from the Spivs and the Cosh boys. Despite the vicious aspect associated with these dangerous youths, no one can dispute that there is a strange underlying level of sophistication often reflected in their extremely smart and flamboyant attire.

June, and concerns were growing about these wayward teenagers. The Evening Times printed this headline, '**MAN WITH AN IDEA TO HELP THE TEDDY BOYS.**' Jim Currie wrote,

'He's called a Teddy Boy, he's sometimes sneered at, sometimes laughed at and often made to bear the blame for social wrongs that were not his doing. We've accepted his type as an odd manifestation in a normal world of bikinis and atom bombs.

I don't know what makes a Teddy Boy. Psychologists may be right when they talk about an exhibitionist that hides a suppressed character or a desire to add brightness to drab lives. You can put away your sympathies and your welfare state attitudes of mind. These lads don't want it. They want something that's modern and bright and in tune with how they feel.

I've been talking to a man who is probably the most successful club organiser in Glasgow and do you know what his opinion is? It's this. "We are talking a lot of tosh about Teddy Boys. We say we want to help them but what has the average youth club got to offer, something that is fifty years behind the times, such as plaster casting and country dancing."

That man is James Muirhead of the famous Maryhill Club. And I knew when he spoke to me he was not just spouting these views to pass the time. No, he thinks we have made the Teddy Boy problem and he also thinks we can solve it. What's the answer? Mr Muirhead thinks he has it in the type of club he operates. Certainly for variety I have never come across anything like it. But Mr. Muirhead isn't just offering advice. He is willing to prove what he says and this is how he is going to do it. On June 21st his clubrooms in Doncaster Street will be open to anyone who is really interested in his problem. Every activity in the place will be staged. Before guests leave Mr Muirhead hopes they will be impressed enough to help him. But it's not just the Teddy Boys who interest the Maryhill Club, they want to encourage every boy and girl in the city who is not attached to some organisation and this is their challenge to the citizens of Glasgow. "Give us your moral support and backing and we will stage our activities anywhere in the city. We are eager to start. We think we have something that will attract the young people."

The Evening News had a youth notes section in their paper. It reported on youth development within the city and could be supportive of organisations that worked with all age groups of young people but they also, in co-operation with the Maryhill Club, ran an event called Youth on Parade. This was a show that originally ran one week a year but now they were taking bookings from organisations who wanted to develop youth work once a month all over the city of Glasgow and the surrounding areas.

Peterson Park Tenants Association took up this offer. At Blairdardie the need for youth work was realised back in 1953. The tenants' association then had been six months old. It was great for the adult community. They had among other things dancing and socials, but there was nothing for the young folk so they opened a youth club one night a week. Shortly after this they started a junior club but it didn't last long, due to the lack of interest from the adults. They were delighted that the Maryhill Club would be presenting Youth in Action on Tuesday 24th June at the Socialist Sunday School Halls in Knightswood at 7.30pm.

Bobby Muirhead and Carol Haldane

131

James was making arrangements for a slightly extended visit to the continent. The Spanish basketball authorities had given the Maryhill team an invitation to play against the Spanish top teams over a ten day period. A hotel in San Sebastian would be headquarters to the club from the 19th July until the 1st August. Then there was a four day tour of Normandy, but first it was off to Cumnock for a two day cycling rally before they left.

30th July, the West of Scotland Cycling Defence Committee sent a letter of thanks to the club. This is a small extract.

'Dear James, Bobby Muirhead and Carol Haldane,

Another Cumnock rally has passed, and thanks to your great assistance and the show of the best club in Britain another success has been added to cycling history. The rally was the most outstanding one of the series up to date, and without a doubt the best cycle rally in Britain. I now give my thanks and the thanks of the committee for coming down again and giving a show second to none in Britain and as such look forward to the next year at Cumnock.'

On the club's return from the Spanish tour, the Evening News printed this headline, **'TO ITALY?'** Jim Currie wrote, *'We have had a successful tour," I learnt from a sun-tanned Mr Muirhead. "We defeated two North of Spain select teams and played matches with other clubs. We never lost a game." The Maryhill Club found themselves having to travel nearly two*

hundred miles to play one game. The club has won far more games than they have lost on the continent and incidentally has done much propaganda work on behalf of British sport into the bargain.'

There was no time to rest. The Youth on Parade seemed to be popular and the Maryhill Club was off to Yoker. The Evening News was hot on their heels with this headline, '**SHE WANTS A HUBBY WHO CAN PLAY THE PIPES**' by Jim Currie.

"Oh, how I would like to have a husband who played the pipes," sighed Hildegard Lambrechts from Belgium after she watched the pipers of the Maryhill Club strut up and down the Spiers Hall in Yoker.'

For a Glasgow audience it would be the most difficult thing to pick out anything in the show and say, "That's my choice." It was all good. But mark the name Cathie Brawley. Cathie is a singer who, to put it in my colleague, Tom Jennings words, "Has forgotten more than most singers ever knew."

It was time for the Maryhill Club to put on their Christmas Revue Show, as they now called it, in Doncaster Street. If you managed to purchase the Evening News on Friday 9th December, priced 2p, then you would have seen the headline, '**THEY'RE RIVALS TO THE TOPPERS, THE TOT-ERS.**' There was a large picture with the words, '*How do you like this chorus line-up? Mind some aren't as young as they used to be.'* There were six gorgeous girls aged four to seven years old. The show opened on Wednesday 15th December until the 22nd. Merry Christmas.

Extract Evening News

1956
BY POPULAR DEMAND

Thursday 12th January and the Maryhill Club had hit the front pages of the Evening Times. The front page contained four pictures of the club members and activities with the heading, **'THERE ARE MORE MARYHILL CLUB PICTURES ON THE BACK PAGE. IN THE MIDDLE PAGES IN ADDITION TO MORE PICTURES, YOU WILL FIND THE EXCITING STORY OF THE MARYHILL CLUB'** by their reporter Donald Macdonald. *'There were pictures of the cycling team, pipe band, archery team, footballers, boys P.T, Indian Club team, concert party, grandparents and much, much more.'*

Extract Evening Times

The centre pages held the title, 'THE COMMUNITY SPIRIT THAT'S OUR SECRET.'

'*The Maryhill Club in Doncaster Street, Glasgow believes that the best way to keep its members is to get them into the club when they're young. That is why this remarkable organisation whose methods are now being copied on the continent, can claim that the present age group of the membership ranges from 2 ½ to 90. There are several instances in which four generations of the same family are on the membership roll. There are at present three members of the mothers' section, whom as girls, held office as captains of the club.*'

The article went on to tell the history of the club and listing all its activities. But there was one other item of great interest in the article and that was of their sporting record. '*It either holds or has held all the Scottish basketball and fencing championships, and a number of football championships and many track cycling and roller cycling championships. At the moment it holds the free standing gymnastic championship for Scotland.*'

Extract Evening Times

136

26th March and a letter of thanks from the Girls Guildry, (which later on became the Girls Brigade), came for the participation of the Maryhill Club in the Guildry's annual display.

4th May and another thank you came this time from the Royal Air Force Association. *'On behalf of the Scottish Area Council I would like to thank you most sincerely for the wonderful performances which the youth club contributed to our Festival Of Re-Union this year at St Andrew's Halls'.* But trouble was brewing.

James was a man of clear vision. He not only worked well with the youths but he seemed to be in tune with their growing needs. But there was a downside to this, which usually involved personal conflict for James from other people who worked in the same field. Old hat, I hear you say? 'Yes,' I reply. But there were times when James seemed to forget that when his club moved forward and provided a track record of success, for others to follow he sometimes didn't give them enough time to catch up. It was becoming a bone of contention especially in the Union Of Boys Clubs, who had been in existence well before James and his club. They greatly resented the man, and whether it was a conscious act or not, he made them feel inadequate at their job.

Extract Evening Times

137

If the officials wished to choose a path of resentment and personal vendettas against him, then that was their choice, but when it interfered with the progress of youth development that was another matter. So on the 2nd May he resigned as chairperson of the union. On the 10th May the Glasgow Union of Boys Clubs officially wrote to James regarding his resignation. This is a small section of the letter.

'It is the desire of the executive that the invaluable advice and work which you have given to youth clubs and to the executive in particular be put on record. The matter of you remaining on the executive, so that union may benefit from your wide experience of youth work has been stressed again and again and I hear with personal gratification that you have agreed to do so. I am sure this will be good news to all who have the real interests of the union at heart.'

The resentment towards James and his club was to grow, and some officials were going to back him into a corner, but for the time being James would play the waiting game.

The club was in full swing. They had already done their annual concert in the March at the St Andrew's Halls and started the Youth on Parade tour with the Evening News. Soon the results of the tour were hitting the headlines. In June the Evening News printed, '**MARYHILL CLUB IN DEMAND AGAIN.**'

'Ayrshire wants to do things the Maryhill Club way but that's not surprising. The famous Glasgow club has had requests for help from the most unexpected places including Egypt, Africa and the continent. And in their usual neighbourly way they try to do as much as they can for others'.

The Ayrshire request came from the Education Department, asking if thirty members could visit the club in Doncaster Street and the reply was, 'We'll come to you.' They did, packing the Kilmarnock Burgh Hall with youth clubs.

This Youth on Parade tour was certainly taking shape as more and more people were taking up the performances. They had already been to Thornliebank and were due next month to go to Springburn and the following month to Arden. The Evening News sang the club's praises in an article called **'MARYHILL YOUTH CLUB RATE TOP MARKS'** by Jim Currie.

Extract Evening Times

This year the club's continental tour was to Denmark. It was a normal part of the Glasgow Fair to see the Maryhill Club and their bus setting off to foreign pastures, but it was to be the strangest reception for them yet.

10th August and the Evening News printed, **'DANES GIVE MARYHILL GIRLS SLOW HANDCLAP'** by Jim Currie.

'The girls of Maryhill Club got the slow handclap from a massed Danish audience and they almost wept. It happened again and again during their request tour of the little island community. But what the Maryhill girls didn't realise that first evening, was that in Danish society the slow handclap was the opposite of what was in Britain. The Danish weren't boo-ing

them off stage they were applauding for more. They had been invited to perform in the town's open air theatre. "The most beautiful I have ever seen," said Mr Muirhead. It seated over 3,000 people but there were people standing at the back. "We finished our show by singing Auld Lang Syne and as we sang the first notes every person in that theatre rose to their feet and sang with us. I'll never forget it."

Extract Evening Times

It was a wonderful memory to bring back to windswept Glasgow. They had just enough time to unpack their bags and it was off to Yoker, to the Speir's Hall for a Youth on Parade with a packed performance of club swinging, high and low bars, dancing and other demonstrations.

2nd November and the Evening News had this headline, **'400 IN GLASGOW SHOW TO REMEMBER.'**

'More than 400 of the best amateur and professional entertainers in Glasgow are preparing to give Glasgow a show to remember in the St Andrew's Halls on Wednesday 21st November. Have you ever seen formation dancing on roller skates or the thrill of a roller cycle race? Several professionals

have joined us for the most unusual variety show in Glasgow. They are led by Bill Paterson's Quartette from the Clyde River Jazz Band. With Bill will be the Kansas City Skiffle group and Johnny Farlane, 'Dambusters Pianist' with the Clavoline Impressionists. Just one bit of advice, get your tickets now'.

Extract Evening Times

24th November and James received a personal letter.
'*Dear Mr Muirhead,*

I was present at your show on Wednesday night and I would like to say here and now how impressed I was. It was typical that the Maryhill Club should put on shows such as this. One thing I did notice was the change of faces of those who took part, there didn't seem to be any of the old school left, however I suppose that's how it goes, the old go as the new fill their shoes. I haven't been up to the club since I left but would still like to consider myself a member. It has been three years now since I joined the police force and I'm still indebted to you Mr Muirhead for the assistance and kindness given to me. Please accept this little gift to the funds, it's not as much as I would like to give but I owe it to the club and to you in particular for what you have done for me. – I will never forget you.
Charles (chic) McGown.'

December had arrived and so had issues in the form of the Glasgow Union of Boys Clubs. Some members were continually accusing James of breaching codes of ethics when working with youths such as extending his club into a community centre which was considered unacceptable. Mr. Muirhead and the Maryhill Club had no right to help set up other youth groups. He was accused of setting up other groups to gain control and that he alone was giving the new youth of today expectations that were causing them to rebel against society.

The breach between the union and James grew as the dispute over the development of the Maryhill Club grew. By the 18th December he had sent his resignation as a committee executive but also withdrew his club from the union. James believed in his club and its members. He was not going to force the club to conform to the union, which seemed hell bent on going backwards in the dealing of youth work to control this new breed of youngster, 'the teenager'.

The club entered into the Christmas spirit with the Christmas Revue Show, before ending the year with their party. James was as confident as ever, nothing stopped, but deep down inside there was a concern that other affiliations might withdraw from the club.

Extract Evening Times

142

1957
ALONE WE STAND

James held his breath in thought of what might come next. There were bound to be consequences for his withdrawal from the Union of Boys Clubs. The club members prepared themselves for the year, working on new routines, training hard and always striving to improve the performances. While at the offices of the Glasgow Union of Boys Clubs there was great debate over Mr Muirhead's letter of resignation.

On the 12th January they sent James a letter.

'Dear Mr. Muirhead,

I am instructed to write and inform you that at the executive committee meeting of the 21st of January the matter of your resignation from the committee was discussed, and after a full hearing was given to the subject, it was agreed that your resignation be accepted. I am instructed also to convey to you the thanks of the committee for all that you have done for the union in particular and for the youth of Glasgow in general.'

James, with a smile, added the letter to his scrap book.

He was now chairman of the Amateur Basketball Association of Scotland. At least they still believed in his abilities. So too did the Burgh of Grangemouth as the town clerk put pen to paper and wrote to James on the 7th March to book the club for their summer entertainment programme. The Maryhill Club had always been popular visitors to Grangemouth. Last year the unfortunate event of a late arrival, due to the bus breaking down, resulted in the performance being cancelled, but this year would be different and he marked them in the calendar for June.

For the last several years the club had taken part in the Interclub display for the Glasgow and West of Scotland Association of Girls Clubs, who shared the same office as the Union of Boys Clubs. The dispute with the boys club was to affect the relationship which the Association of Girls Clubs had with the Maryhill Club and various other clubs. But the Girls

Association still continued to call upon the club and their services as entertainers and athletes but they no longer asked James to run events on their behalf or ask for his advice and training. They would continue for another year, when the executive committee of the Boys Union was rearranged and it became the Union of Mixed Clubs.

The club was as ever preparing for their next events. This time it was the Indian Club team, now Scottish champions, which was asked to display its talents courtesy of George Ingram. There were some final arrangements still to be made for the event on the 20th April.

April 16th and the Scottish Daily Express wrote to James:

'Dear Mr Muirhead,
Pre-match Entertainment, Scottish Cup Final, Hampden Park
Saturday April 20th
Following my letter of April 12th, passes for entry into the stadium are not now necessary, by arrangement with Sir George G. Graham, secretary of the Scottish Football Association. All personnel concerned will be conducted from the Mount Florida Church hall, after they have had their lunch, into the stadium.'

19th October and the Maryhill Club found themselves in the cinema, helping The Mission to the Out-door Blind Glasgow and West of Scotland, who were showing for one full week a film, 'Peter Finch Special' depicting work done on behalf of the blind. The film was to raise money for national and local services. The members of the Maryhill Club were to be in attendance for the week inside and outside the cinema with collecting cans.

26th October. After a long week at the cinema James and the Maryhill Club were preparing for some special visitors from Mauritius. Officially the Republic of Mauritius, this is an island nation off the southeast coast of the African continent. Britain took control of the island during the Napoleonic wars and the island became independent in 1968. The people speak Mauritius Creole, French and English. There is no official recognised language of the island, but English is generally accepted as such. James had always been a good ambassador regarding sport, youth work and development, in this country and abroad. He was only too pleased to help.

This had been a strange year for the club. There were literally no documents or newspaper articles. It was as if James was keeping the Maryhill Club from the limelight, protecting it from those who wished to harm it. This was to be the last year that the Union of Boys Clubs and James would cross paths in the club's history.

There is one young man that we should mention at this point. Let me take you back to 9th April 1939 and the birth of Robert junior. Robert grew up in the traditions of the Maryhill Club as soon as he was old enough. He was going through his paces like everyone else. James and Helen were hard on him so that everyone understood there was to be no favouritism for their son. Robert was known all his life as Bobby. He had become an athlete in his own right, basketball, wrestling, gymnastics, hand balancing, the list was endless. As well as these, he was a performer playing in the club's first skiffle band. He was an excellent drummer. His other duties in the club were coaching gymnastics, balancing, vaulting, high low bars and beam work and the making of scenery. He had an eye for design and colour. His parents thought he should go to art school but Bobby had other plans. He had his own ambition to become a paramedic. Sadly this was not to be for at least a good few years yet so he went to Glasgow School of Art and became an interior designer. He then took up a position as an interior designer in his father's business. He also became the West of Scotland gymnastic champion for several years following.

Maryhill keep fit team

1958-1959
NATIONAL HEIGHTS

10th February and letters and requests crammed the letter box of the Maryhill Club. One such letter was a booking from the Perthshire Agricultural Society. They were getting their booking in early for the display team to perform at the society' annual event on Saturday the 2nd August.

1st April and the Scottish Council of Physical Recreation sent a letter of thanks for the Scottish school boys' exhibition which had been held in the March.

'The club did very well and I am sure they have enhanced their prestige considerably. An amazing number of people must have seen the Maryhill shows. I would like to add a special word of thanks to Bobby who was so willing and competent in assisting. You have a good pupil there to carry on the Muirhead tradition.'

4th August. The Evening News ran the headline, **'BRIDGETON EXPERIMENT.'**

'Because of the lack of qualified leaders for youth clubs in the Bridgeton area, officials of the Glasgow and West of Scotland Association of Mixed Clubs and Girls Clubs arranged a meeting with representatives of churches in the district. The outcome is that a course has just started for potential helpers between the ages of 18 and 25. It is to be held on Tuesday evenings in Barrowfield Church Hall, Bridgeton, under the leadership of Mr James Muirhead. If this experiment is successful other areas may follow.'

James smiled. He had been asked by several representatives of the church to come to the meeting and after much debate James decided to attend. The churches felt that the youth of today should be handled in a way that addressed their needs and a strong leader was essential to guide them, someone with vast experience who could produce instant results, someone who could pass on valuable lessons in life.

14th June and there was a lot of excitement within the club house. For the next few days the Maryhill Club would be playing host to a special foreign royal visitor and his party, whose aim was to develop youth work in his country.

6th September and there was a letter in the post from a rather different type of club, one which James had never crossed paths with until now. It was from the Phoenix Youth Club for Disabled Persons based in Union Street, Edinburgh. Their request was simple enough. They wanted to come and see the Maryhill Club in action, to gain experience to develop their club. This club was to be very different. They weren't to be the kind of club who would take disabled persons out to be entertained; they were going to take disabled persons and show them what they could do, things that everyone else could, such as entertainment, drama, basketball and fencing. James raised an eyebrow at the thought. There were so many forms of disabilities but, never having refused to help in the past, he wasn't going to now and the Phoenix Youth Club was invited along. They were so impressed by what they saw of James' vision on youth work that very soon youth leaders were coming to the club house at Doncaster Street for training.

9th September and the Youth Fellowship was writing to confirm the booking for a performance from the Maryhill Follies at the end of the month and also with a request for a visit to the club with some International Youth Fellowship workers.

11th September and the British Sports Council was again calling on the services of the Maryhill Club for their foreign visitors.

Jig Time was broadcast by Scottish Television on a Friday night. The programme was in black and white and the opening scene was a barn door with a sign saying Jig Time in The Old Barn Ten o'clock. The host was Jimmy Nairn. There was lots of Scottish dancing and singers performing Scottish songs, ballads and lullabies. On the 21st September Jig Time aired live with the Maryhill Club. Bruce McClure was the dance director and he wrote,

'Dear Mr Muirhead,

I am most grateful to you for the help you have given me in supplying the dancers for last Friday's 'Jig Time'.

They entered into the mood of the show just as I hoped they would and I do hope they enjoyed being with us on Friday evening.'

28th October. A special letter arrived in the mail box for James and the Maryhill Club from the Banwaketse Tribal Administration.

'Dear Mr Muirhead,

Although it is a few months after my visit to Glasgow, the memories of the activities displayed by your club still run through my mind. I remember the happy faces of the performers and onlookers and the keen interest taken by all including the youngsters lifting weights.

I have had the papers showing the pictures of some of the club and the articles explaining about the activities of the club, read by some interested people here. I was able to expound on what I had actually seen and heard explained by you and Mrs Muirhead.

The activities of the Maryhill Club have so inspired me that I have adopted them as a role model. We are planning to build a recreational hall next year to conform in most respects to yours. Perhaps you could be good enough to advise me on some improvements.

With all good wishes.
Yours sincerely,
Bathoen ll B.E
Paramount Chief of Banwaketse.'

Now for those of you whose geography is as bad as mine Banwaketse is in Kanye Bechuanaland in South Africa. During the late 19th Century there had been trouble, leading the three main Botswana chiefs to make a strategic pact to seek protectorate status with Britain. The British actually declared a protectorate, first south of Botswana in 1884 to keep out the Boers, and secondly over southern Botswana in 1885 to keep out Germany. Thus on 27th January 1885 the British Protectorate of Bechuanaland under the High Commission for South Africa was established, the British hoping it would be later absorbed into the Union of South Africa. Later in 1966 Botswana received independence with its own president.

November and the Maryhill Follies were off to Dunoon to perform for the National Association of Cycle Traders' annual dinner.

December was here again and this year their Christmas party would be ending on a high note for the Maryhill youths as Scottish Television had broadcast live on the 26th November at St Andrew's Halls, the Maryhill Youth Club on parade. David Webster, from The Scottish Council of Physical Recreation, was an excellent commentator. Highlights were shown that evening at 10.45pm on Scotsport.

BAŃWAKETSE TRIBAL ADMINISTRATION

"Thy Will Be Done"

TEL. ADD.: KGOSI
P.O. BOX 1

...EN II C.B.E.
...UNT CHIEF OF
...NWAKETSE

KANYE,
VIA LOBATSI
BECHUANALAND P...

.../10(174).

B2/LMM.

1st March,

Mr. James Muirhead,
    The Maryhill Club,
        43 Doncaster Street,
            Glasgow N. W.,
                E N G L A N D.

Dear Mr. Muirhead/

I was highly delighted to receive a letter f...
as an expression of good wishes from Mrs. Muirhead...

After seeing and learning how the Maryhill C...
its activities, I came to the conclusion that it w...
impossible for us here to form clubs and expect th...
in the absence of a meeting place. I go on moving...
managed to raise over £3000 for the erection and e...
...nasium hall. Outside this building there is en...
... The only club...

Actual tribal letter

151

14th January. James was sitting in his favourite arm chair. His mornings began much the same, breakfast followed by tea and mail. Opening a letter from the East Kilbride Congregational Church, his thoughts drifted back to the previous May, when he had addressed an assembly of churches and associated church organisations in matters of training and developing potential youth workers in the Glasgow area. He smiled as he read the contents. Now the Rev. James Dey was asking for help in establishing a youth club within East Kilbride Church.

1st February and the club was preparing for a visit from the Edinburgh based Phoenix Youth Club. Their president and club leader, Richard Richardson, was coming in person and he was bringing with him an unusual proposal. Both Richard and James agreed there was a lack of support or proper facilities for disabled youths in Glasgow. By the end of their meeting it was agreed that the Muirheads would host a section of their club for disabled members in association with the Phoenix Club. Without missing a step, Helen and James created their new section of the Maryhill Club.

12th February. A letter, this time from Rev K. K. Lodge of Bonhill, who was the convener of the Congregational Union of Scotland Youth Committee, asking James to attend a youth leadership course on the 18th May and speak for an hour on The Club Night followed by questions and answers.

20th February. The Citizen's newspaper reporter Neil Stuart had these headlines,

'THIS PLAY WILL RUN ON WHEELS.'

'When all members of a drama club are disabled teenagers, many of them in wheel chairs at that, you would imagine that their choice of play to be produced in public would present a ticklish problem. Mr Muirhead who is starting this club for handicapped teenagers has found a very good short play about hospital life in which most of the players will do their acting in wheel chairs. Rehearsal will start with the new club in

the first week of March as well as a drama group. These youngsters, disabled through illness or accident, will have their own choir, handicraft group and concert party and for those who can, there will be a dance class. The club will start with 25 members and will form part of the Maryhill Club. It will be the first of its kind in the west of Scotland. Mr. Muirhead tells me, "Most of these disabled teenagers are lonely and very conscious of their handicaps. Here they will learn to entertain themselves instead of being taken to be entertained." The new club will work in association with the Edinburgh based Phoenix Club.'

The year continued in Maryhill Club fashion with performance after performance as James strove to help more people. Money was becoming tighter. The early sixties were producing a new brand of teenager who didn't want to be tied to a club. They would want to go to a club, do one thing and leave. Slowly youngsters were losing commitment to clubs like the Maryhill.

The next decade was to see many changes. The birth of social work in 1964, the Department of Health and Social Security came into being in 1968. The BBC began to broadcast in colour four hours a week and charged £10 a year for the colour licence fee. Also in 1968 councils began to structure governance for all clubs. Those meeting the new legislation would be eligible for grants. These new teenagers and laws were to be the demise for clubs and the Maryhill Youth Club was to be no exception.

Extract Evening Times

1960-1965
The Demise Of The Maryhill Club

1960

January and the club opened for business as normal, with bookings well into July. There were the usual new routines and performances to perfect.

The headquarters at Doncaster Street was feeling its age. The roof had sprung a leak and after closer inspection it became apparent that the actual fabric of the building was in a poor condition and was slowly rotting away. This was an increase to the burden that James was already carrying. There had been a decline in revenue over the last few years and the businessmen of Glasgow had tightened their purse strings. The Muirheads were feeling the financial burden.

Everything went on as normal as James and Helen kept finances a tightly guarded secret. Even their son Bobby was unaware of the grave situation the club was operating under.

Eleanor McGregor was a club leader. During the day she worked as a tracer in a drawing office and was spending her lunch breaks helping James. *"I remember Jimpsy, as we called him, had an Austin Princess, and I would go with him to collect money which was owed from customers for work his business had carried out. More and more his business was becoming the finances to support the club. We all knew but never said a word; we all just tried do what we could, the club was everything to us."*

1st March. A letter from the Banswaketse tribal administration arrived.

'Dear Mr Muirhead,

After seeing and learning how the Maryhill carries on its activities, I have came to the conclusion that it would be utterly impossible to form clubs and expect them to function in the absence of a meeting place. I go on moving and have managed to raise £3,000 for the erection of a gymnasium hall. Outside this building there is enough ground for tenniquoit, swing, seesaws etc. The clubs I can't afford are archery and an orchestra. I have tried in South Africa for roller cycling outfits without success. I wonder whether you could please describe it for me giving necessary measurements of the materials used. I think I could get a firm here to make them as it is too costly to bring one out to South Africa. The building will be built after the style of yours, separate dressing and shower rooms for boys and girls, kitchenette and store room, collapsible platform wall bars etc. The active clubs are four at the moment and four more wait the erection of the new hall. Once more thank you for your kind thoughts and I'm sure Mrs Gillespie of the British Council will be interested in our achievement as she made it possible for me to visit your club.

> *Kindest regards,*
> *Paramount Chief Banswaketse.'*

Club captain and secretary with James

3rd May. The Muirheads received a letter from a gentleman in Renfrew.

'Dear Mr Muirhead,

You and Mrs Muirhead are most certainly toilers and all your labours will not go unrewarded, for you have been the means of building richly into the characters and lives of very many young and old, something beyond price and value.
May every blessing be yours.

Yours respectfully,
Robert B Laird.'

December and there was a special performance to be given at the Mission to the Adult Deaf and Dumb for Glasgow and West of Scotland.

1961

12th January. The Scotsman had this headline,
'IT'S THE SUCCESS OF THE COUNTRY.'

'Mr. Muirhead should be proud of the 26 years he has devoted to the young people. Does Mr Muirhead then view the present adolescent scene through sentimental eyes? No. He is down to earth in understanding that problems of the 1961 youths are different even from those teenagers ten years ago. Many youths of today are punch drunk with confusion. They have an inferiority complex that shows itself in gangs and drink. If we could manage more clubs like Maryhill in Scotland I feel we would have the answer.'

13th January. A letter of thanks arrived for the Maryhill Club from the Mission to the Adult Deaf and Dumb Glasgow with special regard and thanks for, *'The type of show was one which did not require the gift of hearing and because of this it was very greatly appreciated.'*

The Maryhill Club and STV studios over the years had built up a good relationship. So when TV presenter Larry Marshall presented the Good Neighbours Club, of which Larry was president, it seemed fitting that he should call upon the help and support of James and the Maryhill Club. Last year the club had given a display at the Good Neighbours Anniversary Ball.

30th March. The Evening Times ran this article by Tommy Shields.

'Club president Larry Marshall and many of STV's Good Neighbour screen personalities, who are taking part in this week's 'Stars for Spastics' variety show at the Alhambra Theatre, will be making special guest appearances on the Maryhill Youth Club stand for the next fortnight during the Boys' and Girls' Own exhibition in Glasgow's Kelvin Hall. Host to the STV's stars will be the founder of the biggest youth organisation in Britain, James Muirhead, who is an old friend and ardent member of the Good Neighbours Club.'

This was the opening paragraph.

'James Muirhead, 44 year old managing director of a Glasgow interior decorating firm, is a man with a mammoth plan to open dozens of youth clubs all over Britain based partly on the Good Neighbours Club.'

Also that day another newspaper ran this headline, **'TAKE THOSE WEE BRATS AWAY.'**

'Now Maryhill Club has 800 members. 'If you don't ban those dirty little brats from your Sunday school we will take our children away.' That's the un-Christian-like note James Muirhead got when he was superintendent of a Sunday School in a certain Maryhill Church. "I was banging my head against a brick wall," said Mr Muirhead. "So I stepped out and started the Maryhill Club. If we find that clubs want further help after seeing our demonstrations we can actually supply them staff for a limited period. My wife and son and myself and our section leaders devote at lot of time doing this kind of work. It may be that we are deprived of other pleasures but we think our work is worthwhile and, in any case, we get our reward from the progress we make, we enjoy what we are doing."'

The club performed and demonstrated as normal, but James had changed course slightly. His vision was no longer one club but many. There was a new breed of teenager out there and he was going to capture their imagination and hopefully save his club.

Extract Evening Times

September and reporter Tommy Shields wrote this article with title, '**MARYHILL CLUB SET THE PATTERN.**'

'The Olympia in East Kilbride, Scotland's premier bowling alley and ballroom has been chosen as the operational headquarters of a revolutionary plan to recruit the youth of Scotland into a vast army of Good Neighbours. Last weekend the Olympia was the venue for the first 'experimental' meeting of many East Kilbride teenagers. Such was the enthusiastic response it was decided to go ahead with the formation of the first branch of Scotland's Good Neighbours and Social Club in which youth will play a big part.

Mr Muirhead, the 45 year old founder of the Maryhill Youth Club, the biggest youth and social organisation, is the man behind this most ambitious scheme. It is envisaged that Mr Muirhead's plans will form the basis for an eventual amalgamation between the Maryhill Club and the Good Neighbours Club in a joint effort to expand their welfare services. Although assisting local welfare organisations will form the basis of each club, teenagers of the new-styled Olympia Sports and Games Club will have plenty of time to relax and enjoy themselves, as well as activities such as wrestling, gymnastics, Scottish country dancing, archery and fencing. The active courses will be interspersed with lectures, discussions and pop music jamborees.'

The following week the same report had these headlines, '**IT ALL BEGAN IN A WEE SHOP IN GARSCUBE ROAD.**' *'A mammoth plan to open dozens of Good Neighbour Clubs through Scotland has been launched by James Muirhead, managing director of a Glasgow interior decorating firm and founder of the Maryhill Club. A live wire personality whose motto is, 'getting things done' and lives by the dictum, 'service is the rent we pay for our room on earth,' Mr. Muirhead believes that there are hundreds of girls and boys and old people who throughout Scotland need the Maryhill Club.'*

The Maryhill Club continued performing for events. The corporation of Glasgow was delighted at the performance for their old people's club.

Extract Evening Times

1st March. The Evening Times had this headline,
'FUN AND FITNESS IS THIS CLUB'S CODE.'
'Viewers tonight can sit back in their armchairs at 7.30 this Thursday night and watch more than 500 members of the Glasgow Maryhill Club, the largest youth club in Britain, taking part in a varied 'Parade of Youth' at the St Andrew's Halls in Glasgow. There should be much to please most tastes in this 50 minute display of fun and fitness. The club members range in age from two and a half to twenty and those in the display will be out to prove that keep-fit is as enjoyable as they claim. Among the events to be introduced by David Webster are judo, wrestling, vaulting, mass club swinging, trampoline and a tiny tots' display. The programme is presented by arrangement with the Milk Marketing Board.'

There were to be several television appearances by the club in conjunction with the Milk Marketing Board. In the 1960s there was a television series called Rawhide, starring a very young Clint Eastwood. This was shown every Saturday night at approximately 7pm, and had a large following. So you can image the look of surprise on the faces of the Maryhill Club members when Scottish television decided that the popularity of the Glasgow club required prime television space, and for one night they replaced Rawhide with a performance of the Maryhill Club in action live from the St Andrew's Halls.

Bobby and Carol Muirhead on holiday

1963

This was a difficult year, the club rooms at Doncaster Street were desperately run down, and the Muirheads had been forced to close the top floor of the club, as it was no longer safe for members. James and Helen had sold their home and had rented accommodation in Dumbartonshire, and still they struggled for funding for the club. This was also the last year this famous club was to go abroad. In the summer of this year they had toured Spain.

August and they had finished their tour and the Muirheads were in their bus with forty tired but happy club members. They were beginning their journey from Barcelona heading for home.

Helen Muirhead was in the front of the bus with the driver. James was sitting behind her, other club members were chatting or dozing as the bus drove through Spain when suddenly a car shot across in front of them. The driver tried to manoeuvre the bus out of the way, but it was too late and the vehicles collided. Helen hit the windscreen before being thrown back into her seat. Within seconds she was out of the bus giving commands. The woman in the other vehicle had not been so lucky. She had been thrown through the windscreen.

As Helen was making sure everyone was all right she noticed James was looking rather pale, so she made him sit down and asked one of the boys to sit with him. She was struggling to keep the girls calm. It was only when the bus driver handed her a scarf and said, "Mrs Muirhead, put this against your face, that looks awfully sore," that she realised she had been hurt. In those days windscreens were held in place by a metal trim. Helen had hit the window and gone through the glass. As she was thrown back into her seat the metal rim of the frame had moved and cut her from below her left eye down her cheek to the bottom of her jaw. The club members found themselves stranded in a strange country. Mr and Mrs Muirhead had been taken to two different hospitals. James had collapsed and Helen was in shock. The authorities just left these kids on the side of the road. Not one member spoke Spanish. The only adult with them was the bus driver. The people in the village however were marvellous. They put the club members up for the night and fed them. The British Embassy arranged the next day for the driver and the club members to go home. Bobby Muirhead with his fiancée, Caroline Haldane, had been running the rest of the club waiting for the return of his parents.

It took weeks before Bobby finally traced his parents' whereabouts. Through the British Embassy, he was informed that James had been treated for a collapsed lung and broken ribs and Helen had broken her jaw in several places having received a hundred and thirty stitches. Bobby made his way to Dover as the British authorities were sending his parents home. However communication was poor and Bobby and Caroline were left to play a waiting game for nearly a week at the Dover terminal before the Muirheads finally arrived on British soil safely.

There were no more club nights for James and Helen for a little while as they were confined to their home to rest, but James wasn't giving up. He had stretched himself very thinly on the ground with the Good Neighbours Club, and their accident meant he couldn't continue to progress his work. He searched for new premises writing to all he knew, but to no avail, there was nothing.

There was to be one happy note for this year. James and Helen prepared for their son's wedding to Caroline. The date was set for Saturday, 23rd November. As the day approached an excitement grew, especially with the club members who had been invited to this special day. It seems even this was to be marred. On the 22nd November at 7pm British time, the news that President J.F. Kennedy had been assassinated filled the world with horror.

The bride on her trampoline

August, and James had been given notice to vacate Doncaster Street as it was considered to be in such poor repair that it was unsafe to continue using. Glasgow Council had plans for a new development and the building was earmarked for demolition. James' health was still poor after the accident and he took the decision to sell his business.

11th October, James and Helen had a moment of happiness as they shared with their son and his wife the birth of their granddaughter.

November and James and Helen could do no more. They called together their club members young and old to give them the news that at the end of this year the club would close its doors.

They held their Christmas party in Maryhill style and with great sadness they closed the door on 31 years of the most famous youth club in Britain, the Maryhill Club.

OUR CLUB MEMBERS

Here are some of the photographs which club members have sent.

In 1951 this photograph was taken at Barnes Youth Hostel. These are the members we could identify, Bobby Palethorpe, Alex Donaldson, Jack Hill, Davie McLaren, Jim Harvey, John Robertson, Tommy Kane, Sandy Campbell and Billy Lyons.

In 1954 this photograph was taken at campus Barnes Stirling Back row,? Marie Brawley,? Kathy Brawley, Silvia Taylor and Helen Thomson.

Middle, Margaret McMahon?
Front, ? Rita Murray, ? Margaret Baird and Jeanette Dunn.

This is a list of some of the members. It may not be accurate, but the essentials are there. They were a very versatile bunch, and nobody was limited in abilities, but this is what we remembered.

Maryhill Wheelers.
Billy Bell, Willie and Bobby Palethorpe, Tommy Kane, Jim Harvey, May McNeil (whom later we believe became Mrs Harvey), Alec Bell, Bobby Cochrane, Davey Kane, George Greugh, Tommy Banks, Albert Banks Senior, Albert Banks and Will Skiting.

Gymnasts/Keep Fit etc.
Carol Haldane, Bobby Muirhead, Sadie Gray, Margaret Marshall, Jean Marshall, May Kirkwood, Anne Williamson, Barbara Mills, Moira Loan and Mary McGregor.

Maryhill Follies
Eleanor McGregor, (who later became Mrs Lawlor) Kathy Brawley, Marie Brawley, Ray Fisher, Janet Duff, Rita Murray, Ann Kerr, Jean Dunn and Mary Mclean.

Basketball
Gordon Whitelaw, Eddie Lawlor, Neil Gillies, Tommy Burke. John Ross, Charlie Robertson, Bobby Mills, David Pentlands, George Ramster, Charlie Gray and Ralph Cunningham .

Wrestlers
Willie Baxter, Tommy Macatear, Clayton Thomson, David Pentlands Tommy Burke.
Captain of the girls section was Margaret Kelly 1961
Club Captain Rita Murray 1961.

Eleanor Lawlor (Nee McGregor) Eleanor remembered her days in the club with very fond memories. She was just seventeen years old and the Maryhill Club was off to Denmark that year. One of the dancers couldn't go and she was asked to go instead, but she would have to pay towards the cost of £17.00. They travelled by bus to Dover then drove round Denmark for ten days before returning to Glasgow,

She describes Helen Muirhead as a quiet and caring person, but she was firm and was always so graceful on her feet, even as she marched up and down the hall putting the girls through their paces.

James, or Jimpsy as she called him, was an extremely quiet man, but he always, right till the very end, put all of his time and effort and money into the club. There was a membership fee of 5 shillings a year (25p).

It was during this time that Eleanor met and fell in love with Eddie Lawlor who was a promising basketball player. Later they married, and I believe she became a dance teacher.

Every year they took part in a gymnastics competition in Edinburgh where they did free standing agilities such as club swinging, high low bars and floor work. Eleanor recalled how they always took home the trophy except for one year, when an Edinburgh team turned up dancing with hula hoops. After that the competitions just got harder. She even remembers the Follies' opening song, 'Hello There.'

Eddie Lawlor remembered James and Helen Muirhead with great affection. He said you felt you belonged and they played a big part in your life. He remembers the senior lounge with a telly and knackered old arm chairs, but they had a projector with a 3ft x 4ft screen (television was young then) for film nights. He and his wife remembered when Frankie Vaughan visited the club which he did several times. There was a lot of giggling, especially from the girls. He was a big star then, but he came a few times and watched what the club did before he went over to Easterhouse and worked with the gang problems there.

Tommy Burke was another club member who was proud to be part of this club. *"It was more than that; it was like being part of a big family."* Tommy did a lot of different things, hand balancing, club swinging, gymnastics, trampoline and basketball and he feels being part of this club played a big part in his future. Tommy has gone on to do amazing things. He coaches and teaches others. Many young people have crossed his path and last year he won the over 60s Trampoline Championship. He still goes to various events all over Scotland to demonstrate Indian club swinging.

Willie Baxter recalled near the end of the club time. He had been coaching wrestling over at Bellahouston and he would carry the mats from Doncaster Street on his shoulders to teach these kids in Bellahouston after the club closed. Willie not only coached but was a wrestler in his own right. He was for a few years British amateur champion and held the Scottish titles as well. Even now you will see him coaching or judging at Highland Games and various other venues.

Caroline Haldane recalled she had been going to the Girls Bridge in the church next door, and heard about the youth club. She went in and asked if she could join and that was that. She took part in various activities. She remembered the concert party was hard to get into. It was always in high demand. The Follies worked very hard. At 13 years old she won the title of Scottish Trampoline Champion. The following year the competition was held at the Kelvin Hall along with other events such as weight lifting and gymnastics. While she was doing stretching exercises, one of the weight lifters was practising a power lift and dropped the bar which bounced, catching her in the stomach and putting her through the wall bars. Carol was rushed to hospital with a suspected ruptured spleen but thankfully that wasn't the case, but she never got to defend her title.

There was one thing that surprised Carol. In all the time she was there, even when she grew up and became a leader, she never once heard the Muirheads raise a voice, and they never spoke of other members in front of anyone. If there were ever issues with members, no one ever knew; it was dealt with privately and kept that way. She also remembers that she felt Helen was like a second mother to her long before she had a relationship with Bobby.

The club members would go into hospitals and give displays. She remembered going to Gartnavel General Hospital. The beds and patients were pushed to one side of the ward and they put a trampoline in the middle of the ward and performed. You certainly couldn't do that now.

She had a feeling of self worth doing something for others. It gave her confidence; they were one big happy family. She recalls after her wedding, the papers wanted a picture of her on the trampoline in her wedding dress, but she didn't have it. So the reporter borrowed one that was two sizes too big and asked her to do a couple of summersaults in it. It was impossible, as the dress kept falling off and she got tangled in it so they settled for basic moves. Sadly her marriage to Bobby was to end in 1974.

Bobby Muirhead's memories of the club are very different. He had grown up with the club. When he was very young, his grandfather had been the main carer in his life as his parents were always at the club. By the time he was ten years old Bobby was taking part in most activities. By his 13th birthday he was excelling in basketball, cycling and especially gymnastics. By 16 years of age he held the West of Scotland championship title for men's floor work. After that he found that he was coaching more and more.

What Bobby desired most of all was to join the ambulance service but his parents wouldn't allow him, as that would interfere with the club. It was important to them that Bobby continued coaching and training, so he was allowed to take a position in his father's business.

He has many good memories. One was when they put a skiffle band together. They were all the rage at that time. They had a tea chest, a washboard, guitar and drums and they played,

'You are my sunshine.' It was the only song they knew, and as he recalls the first time they played it in public it was so bad, his father just shook his head in horror. Eventually they won third place in a skiffle competition with 'You are my sunshine.' He doesn't recall them learning anything else.

Bobby had this to say: "Clubs like that don't exist anymore, no-one leads from the front. They all try and lead from behind and that never succeeds. Now you need qualifications to work with youth coaching certificates such as SVQs. It's all nonsense. These can't replace experience which has been handed down from coach to pupil. No matter how much training you do if you can't reach out to these kids, walk their walk and talk their talk you will get nowhere. All my life I have coached and when I had to get a coaching certificate I found out the very people I taught were telling me how to coach. It's ironic really, the only regret I had was that my parents were never around and my life and my future were dictated by the club." Surprisingly enough after all of that, Bobby continued coaching and working with youngsters. After the demise of the Maryhill Club, for another 30 years he ran a gymnastic club and the Meadow Centre Trampoline Club, the latter excelled in the sport and had great recognition as a club and respected athletes. He never did join the ambulance service. Instead he became a first aider, then a paramedic and then he started his own first aid training organisation which he still runs to this day. His whole life has been about helping others. He did more than learn from his parents; he genetically inherited the Muirhead touch.

For the next few years James worked with other clubs, but was always looking for a new venue for his Maryhill Club. In 1966 he approached Jim Currie who was a respected reporter. James had grown to know Jim over the years, and asked him to write a book about the Maryhill Club. Jim agreed and looked over the two large scrap books that James had collected and started work. But after a good few long months, he was at a loss. How would one ever write a story like this? It would take a lifetime to do it justice, and I have to agree. There are so many avenues this book could cover, and maybe one day there will be other volumes, one for the basketball team and its history and the important role it played in its recognition as a sport, or even the Maryhill Follies would be a book on its own, It would be unfair and unjust to James and Helen to leave this story here, so we shall continue.

James and Helen found themselves in the village of Renton, and even though James was fighting for the return of his club, Helen had decided that their life was here and began taking part in the community. Soon both of them were at the local church and James and Helen found themselves back where they started.

James began working within the church and Helen had joined the Girls Brigade. By 1966 James had established a form of Boys Brigade called the Service Cadets within the church. Helen was a leader in the Girls Brigade and by 1967 she had become captain.

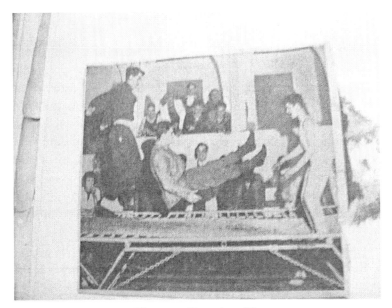

Extract Evening Times

174

Maryhill Wheelers

MARYHILL WHEELERS 1957

World talks of Maryhill Club

"*Evening News*" Reporter

IN a quiet back street in the north side of Glasgow there's a club that has stirred youth leaders all over the globe; in India and Australia they are talking about it and seeking advice.

Meet 40-years-old Mr James Muirhead, dynamic founder of the Maryhill Club, and his homely wife, Helen.

Mr and Mrs Muirhead have had a lifelong interest in church work. It was this that inspired

Extract Evening News

Club Changed a Slum District

BY A "BULLETIN" REPORTER

IT is the kind of street the police used to keep an eye on. Grey blocks of tenements shut out the sky. There is nowhere for the children to play but the roadway and the closes, and some one was always complaining about the

Mrs Muirhead keep a benevolent eye on the proceedings, arbitrate and give advice, while leaving as

CLUB CONC
Maryhill (Gla
Club is very
own concert
has given sev
certs to the
some of the
seen gathered
piano for a

Extract Evening News

Extract Evening News

Maryhill Wrestling Team

Extract Evening News

1967- 1970
Sounds Familiar

This was the start, for the first time since the club closed James was on ground he knew. In May of this year they had something else to celebrate as Bobby and Carol had an addition to the family, their son.

Extract Lennox Herald

The County Reporter printed this article with headlines, **'RENTON REVELS.'**

'The 1st Renton Boys Service Cadets a new uniformed organisation, joined forces with the Girls Brigade on Wednesday and Thursday nights last week to produce a highly

entertaining show 'Renton Revels.' The show was produced by Mr. J. Muirhead who runs the Service Cadets; his wife is the captain of the Girls Brigade. The Service Cadets which exist through their activities to further the kingdom of God on earth has one motto, 'Service is the rent we pay for our room on earth.'

Extract County Reporter

30th April and the County Reporter had this headline, **'RENTON GIRLS ON PARADE.'**

'The 21st annual display of the Renton Old Church Girls Brigade was held in Renton Primary School last week.

It also marked the first display of the recently formed Boys Service cadets. Mr James Muirhead, leader of the cadets, along with the local Brigade Officer, was present at the very entertaining display.'

Then slowly there was an increase of sales of work in aid of the Girls Brigade and the Boys Service Cadets. Then there were a few more shows starring the Renton Revels. It was during this time that James noticed the lack of facilities for the youths of Renton and slowly he began hatching an idea.

1970

20th March. The Lennox Herald had this headline,
'Youngsters on Parade.'

> *'A large attendance of parents and friends were present at the annual display of the 1st Renton Girls Brigade and the 1st Renton Boys Service Cadets in Renton Public Primary School. On Wednesday there was a display of games and marching and dancing and gymnastics by the senior and junior companies.'*

Extract Lennox Herald

26th June. The Lennox Herald ran this headline,
'GIRLS BRIGADE FORMS A BAND.'

> *'The first Girls Brigade band in Scotland has been formed in Renton.*
>
> *In 1966, the 1st Renton Girls Brigade faced a crisis when their membership dwindled to about a dozen, then along came Mrs Muirhead who was well known for her girls' display from Maryhill in Glasgow. Mrs Muirhead worked hard and the numbers are up to eighty. The girls between 11 and 15 meet five*

nights a week and on Sunday much time and effort was directed towards the formation of a bugle band and now that goal has been achieved.'

September and the Muirheads were preparing for a musical show to be held in John Street Hall in Renton in aid of club funds. They had bought new instruments and now they were buying a trampoline.

The Lennox had this headline, '**RENTON REVELS RAISE THE ROOF.'**

'The Renton Revels went into a thunderous finale on Friday night to round off three evenings of foot stomping, hip shaking and musical entertainment, and now the Revels are ready to go on tour for charitable and church organizations. On this showing it looks as if they will be in demand.'

Extract Lennox Herald

185

October and the girls from the 1st Renton Girls Brigade gave a concert in Aitkenbar Primary School.

30th December and the County Reporter had this headline in its middle pages,

'RENTON REVELS ARE RARING TO GO.'

'It's service with a smile for the boys and girls of Renton, for the youngsters of the Service Cadets and the Girls Brigade whose Renton Revels concert show has already made a name for itself are all set to make the big time. Because now the kids are not just a concert show, nor just a band, not just a gymnastic team, from now on they are all three rolled into one. And they are ready to prove it. Mr James Muirhead, who runs the organisation, along with his wife Helen says, "We hope to spread out through the west of Scotland and trampoline, archery and fencing would be added to the programme. It all sounds a bit ambitious but they have done it before. Now the two organisations have nearly 360 members between them and there is something on six nights a week.

Mr Muirhead had this to say, "We want to give the youngsters an aim in life and knowledge of service to the community." "Also," he added, "with the leaning towards a permissive society I feel that our work amongst the modern youngsters, outwith church circles, can be a force to counteract this modern trend of youths to ultimate self destruction."

James had been so miserable when he was forced to give up the Maryhill Club. For a few years he had wandered aimlessly, helping where he could with other groups. It was the youth of Renton that had reminded him of the reason why he had given his all to the Maryhill Club, and now these youngsters needed his help, they needed a club of their own, a sense of belonging and so it began.

Extract Lennox Herald

1971-1980
THE BIRTH OF THE SERVADES

1971

12th March. The Lennox Herald pictured the new Mini Band of the 1st Renton Girls Brigade leading a parade through Renton to the Wyle Park. Also this month, the Girls Brigade and the Boys Services Cadets came together in Operation Bleep. They organised various events and functions to raise money to buy the special bleepers for the elderly in the area who live alone. If they fell or were sick they could activate their bleep. The noise is one that neighbours can easily hear and go to the aid of the elderly. Also the youngsters would regularly go round checking that all is working correctly.

Extract Daily Express

12th June. The Scottish Daily Express printed this headline, **'ESCAPE FROM BOREDOM FOR 300 PUB-SCRUBBING YOUNGSTERS'** by Charlie Mackay.

'The pub with no beer, that's the Black Bull Inn, Renton, in Dumbartonshire's Vale of Leven. The bar has been stripped of its furnishing and the mirrors have gone. On the floor lies a tatty notice forbidding the sale of drink to under 18s. It will be ignored for the Black Bull's only customers will be aged 5 to 16

188

years. The Servades group, under the leadership of James Muirhead and his wife Helen, have rented this disused coaching inn from Dumbarton County Council. The Servades comprises of boys from the Services Cadets which Mr Muirhead himself founded and members of the Girls Brigade'.

These new premises were excellent. There was no café in Renton or anything else for the young people. The upstairs had three reasonable sized bedrooms which would be meeting rooms, a staff room, a kitchen and there was a bathroom. There was also a larger room which was to be used as a café. Downstairs the old lounge was to be a television room, the snug was for records. Volleyball would be played in the back court and the cellar would house table tennis and what had been the main bar would be a games room and discothèque.

28th July and the Servades opened the door to the Black Bull as their leisure time headquarters and they would be using the school gym hall for gymnastics and such like.

The club was running six nights a week and each year in the Vale of Leven Academy they held their Youth in Action annual display. They attended many galas and functions and raised money for different charities. The teenager of this period was more rebellious, many of them preferred a club you went to once a week but still Helen and James maintained their club with 300 members. They ran weekly discos for the teenagers and occasionally they would have a band play. Every Saturday morning there were dance classes in the Black Bull, tap, modern, stage and of course Highland dancing. Club members often put on their own entertainment for friends and parents of the club. Members' songs, such as 'Me and My Shadow' were wonderful comedy acts. Then there were also comedy gymnastic acts with lots of falls and tumbles. The club developed a full marching band, with Majorettes, club swinging as well as keep fit, hand balancing, vaulting, trampoline and gymnastics. There was always something happening, new routines to learn and staging being made. It was a hive of activity.

1973

November, Helen began feeling unwell, James was concerned but when Helen announced that she was too ill to go to the club he knew something was wrong. The doctor had reassured James it was only the 'flu but during the night Bobby had called an ambulance. Helen had pneumonia and had suffered a small heart attack.

Extract Lennox Herald -Girls Brigade

1974

July and another disaster was to strike, this time in the early hours of a Sunday morning. James received a phone call from the Alexandria Police Station, to tell them that their premises at The Black Bull were on fire. The fire had started in the empty building next door and had travelled swiftly. James and his son Bobby could do nothing more than watch as the fire brigade struggled to contain the blaze.

The fire had done more damage than had been realised and Dumbarton County Council made the decision to demolish four buildings, including The Black Bull.

This caused immediate problems for James, as he used the old pub as their new headquarters. They had only been using the gym hall at the primary school three nights a week. That hall was booked now with other events. The Muirheads managed to secure the gym hall at the Vale of Leven Academy for two nights. They had to split the club, seniors trained at the Academy, juniors at the primary school except on Thursday nights; this was Girls Brigade night.

Another problem was looming in the shadows. The Renton Primary School was in need of repair and so was the gym hall. This hall had an upstairs, with a massive kitchen. During the week this upstairs was the school dinner hall and downstairs was the gym. The council made the decision to repair the hall as it was a listed building and to build a new school. Yet again James was searching for new premises.

1975

11th October and James and Helen had a special event to attend. One of their club members, a wonderful gymnast and a leader of the Servades, Fiona Crawford, was getting married to their son, Bobby Muirhead.

Extract Lennox Herald

1977

Mrs Alexandrina Cousins was the president of the Servades and her residence was Dalmoak Castle, Renton. She was holding an April Ball in the castle to boost funds for the Servades. Many businesses helped by giving goods to the grand raffle, and acceptance of invitations were flying in.

1978

Mrs Cousins was preparing for yet another ball. Last year's event had raised a grand total of £300 for the club and invites were already in the post. Sadly before the event Mrs Cousins took very ill and shortly after retired from her position as club president due to failing health. Help was at hand when Dumbarton's Lyons Club saved the day with a cheque for £150 for the Servades' funds.

1979

An awards ceremony was held at the Academy. Parents watched proudly as the club members gave a short display followed by presentations. Servade of the year went to Sally McCourt, Balloch, and runner up went to Mary McGeachy, Renton.

Other presentations went to Marie Flynn, Balloch, Sandra Tracy, Ladyton and June Smith, Brucehill.

James and Helen moved from Dalquhurn Villa, Renton , to 40 Cook Road, Haldane. This is where they maintained a lease for the Haldane Primary School Hall. It was ideal for the Servades and with the closure of Renton's gym hall the timing was perfect.

Extract County Reporter

1980

James was now sixty six years old, and an active member of the community. He was in the church, on the community council and involved with groups such as Balloch/Loch Lomond Clean Up Community.

The Servades junior section was established in the Haldane Hall on a Wednesday night and the senior sections were held Mondays and Tuesdays at the Academy. The annual shows were spectacular. They added a mini circus to their programme of events. The Servades were in demand all over Dumbartonshire, with indoor and outdoor events as well as venues further afield.

This year the annual Youth in Action display was as spectacular as ever with the participation of the Scottish trampoline team, one of whom was British gold medallist Lorraine Carbeth. The crowd gasped and ooh-ed as the team reached roof heights in twists and double somersaults.

Over the last ten years the Servades had become permanent attractions at the Renton's gala day and at Levengrove Park as well as fitting in performances at Leven Cottage Home and Willox Park home. They also helped raise monies for the Lyons clubs and various other charitable organisations, not forgetting church fetes.

Helen and James relaxing

Servades Annual Display

1981- 89
The Decline of an Era

These are the last few years of dedicated youth work in Muirhead fashion. There were plenty of grants available to various groups and clubs. The Muirheads yet again found themselves in the position. "It's the only one of its kind in existence,' said James. All clubs at this point were single purpose. James was struggling for funds; there wasn't a grant in existence for a multi purpose club.

Servades outdoor display

The Servades with all their devotion, went on as normal, performing up and down Scotland as well as at local engagements, but that too gradually phased out as it was too costly to travel with teams and they were restricted to venues they could afford.

Local events were on the increase. Some were in the strangest of places. The Lennox Herald published pictures of the Servades in action at Balloch Castle, well, rather more a hand balancing act inside the castle or in the back garden of an old folks' home and the audiences loved every performance.

Helen and James and era of youth work

1987

23rd of July and James and Helen celebrated 50 years of marriage, that's half a century. James Muirhead had opened his doors to his first ever club fifty four years ago and for fifty-three years of them Helen had been by his side and just as devoted to working with youths. There was much to celebrate.

1988

Dumbarton District Council and many other authorities were in financial predicaments and the decision was taken to increase the price of school halls. Letting was to be £15 per hour plus 1 hour for opening and closing to cover janitor costs. James was horrified. He needed £135 a week. That came to £4,860 a year. So yet again they were fighting for survival.

April. Youth in Action's annual display was outstanding, and they raised enough revenue to sustain the club. James was feeling the pressure and collapsed at the display. After a few days in hospital he was back to his normal self but the doctors were unhappy. James was suffering from exhaustion. He had to slow down, after all he was now eighty-one years old. So at the Christmas party the decision was taken to close the clubs. A small committee in Haldane, who ran the Mill Community Hall, offered its service to The Servades. Unfortunately it was too small for the entire club but he could still run the junior section.

Extract Lennox Herald- The Anniversary

April and The Servades put on their final display at the Academy and there was a full turn out of parents and friends, and the senior section was no more.

There was one other event. Bobby and Fiona were helping the Meadow Centre on a Friday night and they were running recreational trampoline evenings.

8th February and the Lennox Herald ran a small article with the headline, '**New Trampoline club to open.**' *'Bobby Muirhead and his wife Fiona will be running a trampoline club every Wednesday evening in the Meadow Centre.'*

Bobby and Fiona worked hard with the trampoline team. Members of the Servades migrated to the trampoline club. So from time to time there were displays from both the Meadow Trampoline club and the Servades gymnastic team. Annual displays took part in Haldane Primary School by the junior section of the Servades with a little help from the Servades gymnastic team. The Servades junior section gave displays locally as before and their club swinging was always in demand and continued to work quietly until 1992.

Meadow Centre Trampoline Team

For Bobby and Fiona however, their club grew from strength to strength. The club after only three months had come fourth in the first competition. It wasn't long before these club members were out washing cars or giving performances to raise money for competitions.

1990

Hazel Mcfarlane, Claire Cassidy, Catherine Quinn, Gillian Matheson and Lisa Palmer were winners at a Barrhead competition. The team brought home gold, silver and bronze medals.

Meadow Trampoline Club

21st March Lindsay Allison won a silver medal at Edinburgh. Then they all brought home silver too, a bronze and gold from Aberdeen later this year. They ended their first year on cloud nine as they took the Scottish championships by storm. In the novice events they took gold and silver, and in the intermediates they took silver and bronze. This prestige format continued until 1992.

Meadow Trampoline Team

1992 The Lennox Herald held this headline, **'Tribute to Jimmy Muirhead.'**

'One of the Vale's best loved citizens has died at the age of 85. Jimmy Muirhead, founder of the Servades and former chairman of the Vale of Leven Community Council, died in the Western Infirmary, Glasgow on Friday. He was cremated in Cardross on Wednesday.

Jimmy who lived at 40/2 Cook Road leaves behind a wife Helen and a son Bob. He began his lifelong work with young people in 1934 when he and Helen established the Maryhill Youth Club. They moved to Balloch and formed their famous Servades group in the Vale of Leven. The voluntary organisation for girls became a byword for their annual display and for fund raising efforts.

Part of the club became the Meadow Trampoline Club coached by Mr Muirhead's son, Bob and his wife Fiona. They wear the same black and gold colours of the Servades and the Maryhill Club.

Bob said, "My father's work is living on and he was very proud when the Meadow Club became Scottish champions. He gave his whole life to community service; no one person could have done more or lived more. Renton and the Vale of Leven have lost a friend. Wherever he was needed he was always there."

Jimmy had chaired the Vale of Leven Community Council and he was active in the Dumbarton Festival and the Balloch/Loch Lomond clean up communities and Jamestown Parish Church.

James had broken his knee in the May of that year, and had to be taken to the Western Infirmary, where his leg was placed in traction. James took ill with a respiratory infection, but other complications soon surfaced. Helen could not continue without James by her side and she took the decision to close the club at Christmas that year. Helen continued on in life until she died peacefully in Dumbarton Cottage Home in 1997 surrounded by her family.

THE ENDING

Writing this book was the hardest thing I have ever done. It has been an emotional voyage of exciting adventures and yet filled with much sadness.

Through this journey of the Maryhill Youth Club I asked several times what made this club unique and now we have the answer, it was James and Helen Muirhead.

James had a vision of a better future for all youngsters, one full of hope and confidence for them to believe in themselves. He also wanted to have Maryhill Clubs all over Britain and in a way that happened as each club member took with them a small part of the Maryhill Club. Some, like Willie Baxter and Tommy Burke, made life choices because of the time they spent in the Maryhill Club, and ended up teaching others, and in turn, have influenced the paths of hundreds of people. It may not be what James had imagined, but he did leave us his legacy of youth work that even now we could learn from.

It wasn't until after the deaths of James and Helen, that one realized just what the Maryhill Club and the Servades had meant to them; they had been so dedicated to the youths they helped they gave their all. They spent every penny they had, all that was left were two scrap books, and a big pair of shoes that I can't imagine anyone else could fill.

I would like to thank all of the Maryhill Club members who sent pictures and shared their stories with me for this book. To those who gave me the inspiration to finish it, but also allowed me to experience a special part of my grandparents' life. You all brought it alive for me, especially Tommy Burke and Willie Baxter.

I would also like to thank my dad, Bobby Muirhead, for all his help and support, and the hours of phone calls he had to endure when I was excited over new discoveries about the Maryhill Club. He would reply, "Yes darling, I know I was there" or, as I read each chapter endlessly to him, then I would change it all.

Also I would like to thank the Scottish Basketball Association, especially Danny Kay, and his heart warming stories of my grandfather. My favourite was when he told me that there was once a James Muirhead cup for women's basketball. Sadly it was mislaid. David Webster was originally from the S.C.P.R and his kind words I quote, "I remember your Granddad very well. He was a great man; I enjoyed working with him and admired the wonderful work he did. One of his sayings has had a positive effect on me throughout my, now long, life. I have used it often." This is the title of this book.

The Serrades demonstrate their gymnastic skill before an audience of 200 at Vale of Leven Academy.

Extract County Reporter

Servades in action

It was all a matter of balance and these Servades had it organised to perfection.

Servades outside in action

Sally ch

Young gymnasts go through their paces as the crowds in Levengrove Park watch.

Extract County Reporter

Fiona Muirhead

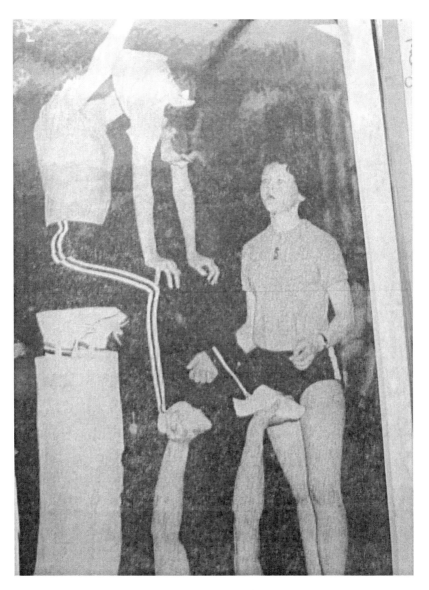

Servades Hand balancing Team

Servades perform

Audiences gasp at Servades in action

Renton Revels training at St Johns Hall

Extract Lennox Herald - Helen and James

Extract Lennox Herald

High in the air at St George's Square